HENLEY-ON-THAMES

MARTIN ANDREW is an architectural and landscape historian and writer on outdoor matters; he is the Conservation Officer for Wycombe District Council in Buckinghamshire. He specialises in the landscape of lowland England, and combines his love of history, landscape and architecture in his writing. Since 1978 he has lived in Haddenham in Buckinghamshire with his wife and children; he is a keen long-distance walker and enjoys riding his classic motor-cycle round the country lanes of the Chilterns. Martin knows Henley well and in the 1980s taught evening classes for Oxford University on the architecture of Henley and the surrounding Chilterns. He was born in Doncaster, but spent most of his childhood in Ealing and Carshalton in Surrey. After university he worked for the Greater London Council's Historic Buildings Division, Buckinghamshire County Council and Salisbury District Council before joining Wycombe District Council in 1990.

YE OLDE XVI CENTURY ELIZABETHAN HOUSES c1955 H73080

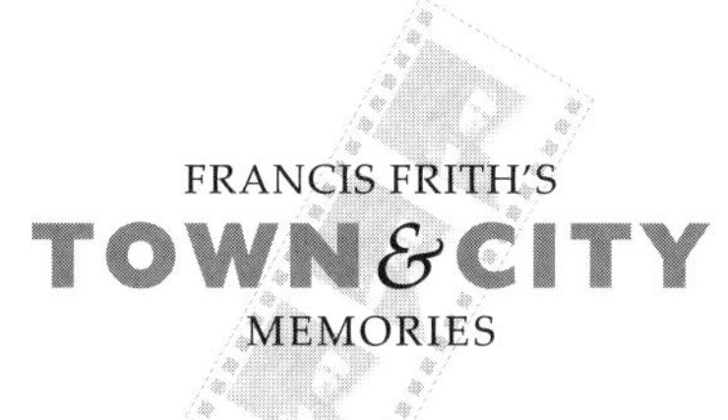

HENLEY-ON-THAMES

MARTIN ANDREW

First published as Henley-on-Thames, A Photographic History of your Town
in 2001 by Black Horse Books, an imprint of The Francis Frith Collection
Revised edition published in the United Kingdom in 2005 by
The Francis Frith Collection as Henley-on-Thames, Town and City Memories
Limited Hardback Edition ISBN 1-84589-055-8
Paperback Edition ISBN 1-85937-990-7

British Library Cataloguing in Publication Data

Henley-on-Thames
Town and City Memories
Martin Andrew

The Francis Frith Collection®
Frith's Barn, Teffont,
Salisbury, Wiltshire SP3 5QP
Tel: +44 (0) 1722 716 376
Email: info@francisfrith.co.uk
www.francisfrith.co.uk

Aerial photographs reproduced under licence from Simmons Aerofilms Limited
Historical Ordnance Survey maps reproduced under licence from Homecheck.co.uk

Printed and bound in England

Fı ... HENLEY-ON-THAMES, THE BRIDGE 1899 ...

Every atte... has been ... terial.
We will be ... ns not
credited ... on.

AS WITH ANY ... Y BEING
CORRECTED ... ION ON
OMISSIONS OR INACCURACIES

FRANCIS FRITH'S

TOWN & CITY MEMORIES

Contents

FRANCIS FRITH

THE MAKING OF AN ARCHIVE

Francis Frith, Victorian founder of the world-famous photographic archive, was a devout Quaker and a highly successful Victorian businessman. By 1860 he was already a multi-millionaire, having established and sold a wholesale grocery business in Liverpool. He had also made a series of pioneering photographic journeys to the Nile region. The images he returned with were the talk of London. An eminent modern historian has likened their impact on the population of the time to that on our own generation of the first photographs taken on the surface of the moon.

Frith had a passion for landscape, and was as equally inspired by the countryside of Britain as he was by the desert regions of the Nile. He resolved to set out on a new career and to use his skills with a camera. He established a business in Reigate as a specialist publisher of topographical photographs.

Frith lived in an era of immense and sometimes violent change. For the poor in the early part of Victoria's reign work was a drudge and the hours long, and ordinary people had precious little free time. Most had not travelled far beyond the boundaries of their own town or village. Mass tourism was in its infancy during the 1860s, but during the next decade the railway network and the establishment of Bank Holidays and half-Saturdays gradually made it possible for the working man and his family to enjoy holidays and to see a little more of the world. With characteristic business acumen, Francis Frith foresaw that these new tourists would enjoy having souvenirs to commemorate their days out. He began selling photo-souvenirs of seaside resorts and beauty spots, which the Victorian public pasted into treasured family albums.

Frith's aim was to photograph every town and village in Britain. For the next thirty years he travelled the country by train and by pony and trap, producing fine photographs of seaside resorts and beauty spots that were keenly bought by millions of Victorians.

THE RISE OF FRITH & CO

Each photograph was taken with tourism in mind, the small team of Frith photographers concentrating on busy shopping streets, beaches, seafronts, picturesque lanes and villages. They also photographed buildings: the Victorian and Edwardian eras were times of huge building activity, and town halls, libraries, post offices, schools and technical colleges were springing up all over the country. They were invariably celebrated by a proud Victorian public, and photo souvenirs – visual records – published by F Frith & Co were sold in their hundreds of thousands. In addition, many new commercial buildings such as hotels, inns and pubs were photographed, often because their owners specifically commissioned Frith postcards or prints of them for re-sale or for publicity purposes.

In order to gain some understanding of the scale of Frith's business one only has to look at the catalogue issued by Frith & Co in 1886: it runs to some 670 pages. By 1890 Frith had created the greatest specialist photographic publishing company in the world, with over 2,000 stockists! The picture on the right shows the Frith & Co display board on the wall of the stockist at Ingleton in the Yorkshire Dales (left of window). Beautifully constructed with a mahogany frame and gilt inserts, it displayed a dozen scenes.

POSTCARD BONANZA

The ever-popular holiday postcard we know today took many years to appear, and F Frith & Co was in the vanguard of its development. Postcards became a hugely popular means of communication and sold in their millions. Frith's company took full advantage of this boom and soon became the major publisher of photographic view postcards.

Francis Frith died in 1898 at his villa in Cannes, his great project still growing. His sons Eustace and Cyril continued their father's monumental task, expanding the number of views offered to the public and recording more and more places in Britain, as the coasts and countryside were opened up to mass travel. The archive Frith created continued in business for another seventy years. By 1970 it contained over a third of a million pictures of 7,000 cities, towns and villages. The massive photographic record Frith has left to us stands as a living monument to a special and very remarkable man.

This book shows Henley-on-Thames as it was photographed by this world-famous archive at various periods in its development over the past 150 years. Every photograph was taken for a specific commercial purpose, which explains why the selection may not show every aspect of the town landscape. However, the photographs, compiled from one of the world's most celebrated archives, provide an important and absorbing record of your town.

ST MARY'S CHURCH: THE HEART OF THE MEDIEVAL TOWN

A church in Henley is first mentioned in 1204. The present church is dominated by its fine tower, which is believed to have been built for John Longland, Bishop of Lincoln, in the 1520s - stylistically this seems highly likely. The churchyard extended further into the road until the 1780s, when the causeway to the bridge took out some of the churchyard. The church has the Red Lion, a medieval inn, between it and the bridge, and to the west is Hart Street, which contains many pre-1700 timber-framed buildings.

THE CHURCH c1965 H73072

An Historic Market Town & Port

Far Right:
Hart Street, St Mary's Church c1955 H73007

Below:
The Church and the Red Lion c1965 H73062

In 1675 Richard Blome wrote of Henley that 'its inhabitants, which for the most part are Bargemen or Watermen, gain a good livelihood for transporting of Mault, Wood and other Goods to London'. He was echoing what England's first topographical historian, William Camden, had written nearly a century earlier in 1586: 'the greatest part of the Inhabitants are Bargemen, and live principally by carrying wood and corn to London by water'. Unhelpfully, he also added that 'this town has nothing ancient to boast of'. Most people's image of Henley in modern times could not be more different: the colourful Regatta crowds swirling like peacocks along the banks of the River Thames or on crowds of small boats; champagne picnics, boaters and striped blazers; and for the rest of the year a comfortable middle class market town with a number of speciality shops, including superior clothes shops, delicatessens, antique shops and art galleries.

In fact Henley, like Marlow some 8 miles downstream, grew up in the Middle Ages, its prosperity largely based on trading locally-grown commodities down river in barges to London along the River Thames; it was very much a workaday town. It was a combination of Chiltern topography and the river's course that moulded the town and provided the circumstances for its success. Chalk ridges come close to the river on both banks. A spur from the Chilterns on the Oxfordshire bank reaches close to the river, descending steeply to the market place and offering some protection from floods. On the Berkshire bank the chalk descends very steeply down White Hill to the flat river valley, here a mere 600 metres or so wide. The river curves into the Oxfordshire bank, keeping the water moving and deep, which proved ideal for the wharves that grew up along the banks. Even more crucial was the decision to throw a bridge across the river at this point, with a causeway from the bank crossing the riverside meadows to the White Hill, whose steepness was a problem until the 18th century.

There seems little evidence of a settlement at Henley before the Norman Conquest, although when the old Regal Cinema in Bell Street was demolished, excavations in 1993 found evidence of Roman buildings, possibly a small farm, and Roman coins and a few other artefacts have been found in other locations within the town. There is also evidence that Grim's Ditch, that great Anglo-Saxon linear boundary earthwork, reached the Thames from the

Rotherfield Greys direction along the line of Bell Street, for a deed of 1591 refers to 'a half acre of land in Bell Street between an orchard and a ditch called Grymes Ditch'. This may have influenced the laying out of the town some time in the early 12th century; the Grim's Ditch earthwork formed a convenient northern boundary for the new town.

Henley is not mentioned in the Domesday Book of 1087, a fact which is described by the Henley historian J S Burn in 1861 as 'a singular circumstance'. The first written reference to Henley is in a charter of King Stephen which is described as 'Apud Henlei' - that is, the charter was granted while the King was in Henley. This charter, granting a mill at Headington near Oxford, is dated to 1135. The next known reference is found in the Pipe Roll, the Royal expenditure rolls, for 1179: it shows King Henry II buying the land of Henley 'ad facienda edeficia', for making buildings.

This is all well and good, but fragmentary. It seems from other records that the town slowly emerged to borough status by about 1300, although it was described in 1199 in a charter of King John as 'the town and manor of Henley'. In 1232 there is a reference to the bridge and its chapel of St Anne, which was actually built on the bridge, a common medieval practice; a similar chapel can still be seen at St Ives in Huntingdonshire. Other hints include a paving grant in 1205, and evidence about the reference to the bridge in 1223 for its repair with wood granted from the royal forest of Windsor. To repair a bridge, it must already exist; and indeed excavations on the Berkshire bank in 1984, before the fine Henley Royal Regatta building was built, found two stone arches of the old bridge. Architecturally they were of late Norman character; the Oxfordshire bank has another stone arch in the cellars of the Angel pub. The central spans were certainly

An Historic Market Town & Port

EXTRACT FROM BARBER'S GAZETTEER OF ENGLAND & WALES 1895

Henley-on-Thames, a municipal borough and market-town in Oxfordshire. The town stands on the Thames, at the boundary with Berks, near the boundary with Bucks, at the terminus of a branch railway on the GWR, and under the Chiltern Hills, 7 miles NE by N from Reading.

of timber after a rebuild in 1483, and the famous paintings of Henley by Jan Siberechts, painted about 1690 and now in the National Gallery, show the timber bridge.

Although in 1279 Henley is described as a hamlet of Benson with a chapel, by 1297 the Earl of Cornwall's revenues include the tolls of markets, of a fair and income from a guild of no less than 46 merchants; in 1300 rent is being paid for burgages, the long narrow plots that line the streets of a medieval market town. Although the town may not have achieved formal borough status until late in the 13th century, it clearly had all the normal features of a borough, and its guild of merchants had been approved in 1269. During the 13th century Henley obviously grew apace: by 1290 a quarter of the grain supplied to the whole of London was shipped through Henley from the corn belt of the Chilterns, and in around 1300, 24 London commoners or merchants traded in Henley. The trade was in flat-bottomed barges, which tied up at the wharves north and south of the bridge; Henley stood where the medieval Thames ceased to be shoaly and divided into narrow channels amid numerous islands upstream. The barges brought back cargoes for the town and its surrounding areas, such as the salt fish referred to in a letter of 1476 from William Somer, a bargeman, who also added that it took four to five days to haul the barges back upstream from Queenhythe in London; presumably travelling downstream was considerably quicker. By 1377 the town had 377 taxpayers, which put it ahead of such towns as Thame, Richmond in Yorkshire, Devizes and Market Harborough.

The parish church, whose 16th-century west tower so dominates views of the town, particularly from the river, has some 13th-century work, which probably ties in with the granting of indulgences in 1272 for those who contributed to its rebuilding and repair. An indulgence remitted a number of days in Purgatory, the anteroom

MEDIEVAL, TUDOR AND GEORGIAN HART STREET

Hart Street was the main street of the early medieval town. It is wide, although until the mid 18th century there were encroaching buildings in the Market Place and in Hart Street as far west as the Catharine Wheel. At the east end, opposite the church, there are two good timber-framed houses, one with two storeys of jetties. The lower one was the birthplace of William Lenthall in 1591. He was the Speaker of the Long Parliament that sat from 1640 to 1653, spanning the Civil War and the start of Cromwell's Protectorate. The White Hart, which gave the street its name, probably dates back to the 1390s. In its yard were galleries, formerly open, from which patrons could watch bull-baiting and cock-fighting.

YE OLDE XVI CENTURY ELIZABETHAN HOUSES c1955 H73080

Below: THE COURTYARD OF THE WHITE HART HOTEL c1955 H73042

Right: HART STREET c1965 H73079

to Heaven or Hell after death, and was an immensely popular fund-raiser in medieval Europe. The earliest reference to a church is 1204, but nothing as early as this survives. The earliest town official was the Warden of the Town or Keeper of the Guild; their names are known from 1305 onwards - Robert Stokes was the first. The title was changed to Mayor in 1526 by a charter from Henry VIII. The Warden, later Mayor, had two bridgemen, ten aldermen and sixteen burgesses, a situation that lasted until reforms in 1883.

Having established the evidence for the growth of the town, I now want to move on to its physical shape and growth up to the mid 19th century. Soon after that time, the Frith photographers arrived to record the town; they give us a fascinating sequence to show the changes from about the 1870s to about 1965. There is much continuity, unsurprisingly, with the street pattern of the historic core of the town largely established by the mid 16th century. Physical growth and expansion thereafter was minor, only accelerating after the arrival of the railway. Major change after that saw the disappearance of the trading town and its change to its present role as a pleasure, tourism and local shopping town serving a middle class hinterland, and as a commuter town.

The town appears to have been laid out along Hart Street, with development along both sides of the south part of Bell Street and

the north part of Duke Street and along the river bank. Expansion followed; by 1200 it is thought that New Street had been laid out to the north, with housing and buildings on both sides. To the south, Friday Street was developed, and in the west development climbed westward; the market place was laid out and Bell Street was developed further north. Along the river, wharves spread north and south as well. However, the town was still remarkably compact, expanding by about 1560 only westwards up Gravel Hill and northwards to Northfield End - the plots were newly laid out in one of the town's great medieval fields.

The medieval plan is virtually intact, and there are quite a good number of medieval, Tudor and 17th-century timber-framed buildings lining the streets, many disguised behind later front elevations or encased in Georgian brick. Some timber-frames are modern facings and not to be trusted; these include the one to the north elevation of the Angel, or 40 Hart Street, now Caffe Uno. The parish church is the most obvious medieval building. Its great west tower was built for John Longland, Bishop of Lincoln after 1520, when the diocese still reached as far south as the River Thames. Longland was a native of Henley, and tradition has it that he was born in the house that preceded the Georgian Longlands by the church. Behind the church is the Chantry House, a medieval timber-framed building, which

An Historic Market Town & Port

THE MEDIEVAL AND LATER RIVER PORT

The riverside on either side of the bridge was lined with wharves, warehouses and inns until the 19th century. Some early buildings survive in recognisable form, such as the Old Granary, the black gable behind the cars in the view looking towards the bridge (H73057, page 18). The New Street and Friday Street houses (the latter can be seen in a dilapidated state behind the RAC man) are part of the late medieval and Tudor fabric of the town. In the foreground of the 1890 view is the last survivor of the timber wharves at the right, which were soon after replaced by houses.

dates from about 1400; it was probably given to the church by one of the town's prosperous merchants. It became the grammar school during the 16th century. Its two upper stories are now used by the parish, and its lowest is used by the Red Lion.

There are many other timber-framed buildings in the town, the finest being the ranges opposite the church on the south side of Hart Street. These include Speaker's House and No 48 next to it. The former is called Speaker's House because, as a plaque records, the Speaker of the Long Parliament, William Lenthall, was born in the house in 1591. Others include the White Hart Inn, the oldest recorded inn in the town; it was mentioned in a Court Roll in 1429. Bearing in mind that the white hart was the badge of Richard II, it may date back to the 1380s or 1390s. It has much timber-framing, and an open gallery along the east side of the inn yard, now enclosed; it was noted in the 18th century for its bull-baiting and cock-fighting.

Some of the skeleton of the old town is exposed along the street front: for example, The Granary along Riverside, and the ranges turning the corner into Friday Street, Barn Cottage, Friday Cottage and Old Timbers, all now restored but important relics of the town and its trade. In New Street there are several old timber-framed houses, some concealed by render, such as

HENLEY RIVERSIDE 1890 27193

the 15th-century one at the corner with Bell Street, and others exposed, such as Anne Boleyn and Tudor Cottages, also 15th-century (the Anne Boleyn name is a later fancy). There are old houses in Bell Street (some are concealed, like No 76, which has a medieval open hall of about 1400), and in Market Place, where the most obvious is Gabriel Machin's the butchers with its elaborately-patterned timber bracing. Plotting the buildings with timber-framing (either visible or concealed, like the rear wing of the Red Lion) gives a good idea of the extent of the town that grew up trading along the Thames with its many inns and timbered buildings.

The original market house and guildhall have long gone. In the 18th and 19th century, the face of the town changed; but the change was a cosmetic one, concealing the gnarled, aged faces of the buildings of earlier years. In the 18th century the town added a role as a major coaching town to its river commerce, and its inns grew in size and number to cope. Henley was a day's coach journey from London, and it was on an important north-south route as well. Several Turnpike Trusts transformed the road system to Henley's benefit: the Hurley Trust, which improved the route from Henley to Maidenhead, the Reading and Hatfield Trust, which passed through the town, and the Dorchester Road Trust, from Henley to Oxford. Many inns adapted to the new trade, including the Catharine Wheel, an inn established by 1499, the White Hart, and the Red Lion, which ensured themselves a new lease of life by serving travellers from much further afield. The Red Lion, situated by the bridge and probably dating back to 1531, was itself mostly rebuilt in the mid 18th century with up-to-the-minute Georgian facades and sash windows.

The first regular coach service to London had been established in 1717. Originally it ran twice a week from Henley's White Hart to the White Horse in Fleet Street, setting off at 6 am and reaching its destination that evening, and returning 'with a good coach and six able horses perform'd (if God permit)'. With turnpike improvements, the time for the journey reduced; there were soon many coaches taking in Henley, at one time nearly twenty.

The 18th century also saw a town of tradesmen, wharfingers and bargees gradually transform into a town with prosperous and fashionable houses, some occupied by gentry, others by tradesmen rising into the middle classes, such as brewers and corn merchants. Their smart new houses, in fashionable brick with timber modillion eaves cornices and box sash windows, denote the earlier Georgian phase of this change; examples from this period include the Old Rectory along Riverside, the refronted Old Armistice west of the church, Simmons and Sons in Bell Street, or the range of good houses along the north-east side of New Street. Many others followed, reflecting the economic well-being of the town until the 1830s; some have parapets, like Longlands of about 1720 near the church, while Georgian houses appeared in Northfield End, including Countess Gardens of about 1740, which still has its original external ground floor window shutters.

An Historic Market Town & Port

Pigot and Co's National Commercial Directory, published in 1830, gives an interesting snapshot of the town just before its rapid decline (the building of the Great Western Railway killed both the commercial river trade and the coach trade at one fell swoop as a result of by-passing Henley). 'Henley, a market town, and one of the neatest, cleanest, and most respectable in the County ... is exceedingly pleasantly situated on the west side of the river Thames'. Commenting on the town's appearance, the Directory says that 'its whole appearance [is] indicating recent improvements, and bearing evidence of the good taste of its inhabitants. The town hall is a considerable ornament to the town, and the market-house is a commodious and well constructed building'. It also describes the town's then economic base: 'a considerable trade is carried on from hence to London, in corn, malt, flour and timber; there is also a considerable manufactory for silk, and another near the town for paper. The inns here are respectable and comfortable; the principal commercial house is the White Hart'.

Above: New Street c1955 H73503

Right: The River c1955 H73057

PARROTT
MOTOR LAUNCHES

ELIZABETHAN HOUSES, FRIDAY STREET
c1955 H73018

The reference to the Town Hall is to the one erected in 1795 to the designs of Alderman Bradshaw to replace the earlier one he demolished. The town also acquired that other symbol of Georgian respectability and status: Assembly Rooms, in Bell Street.

This introductory chapter can only skim the surface to set the scene for what could be termed the photographic portrait of the town contained in the next five chapters. I have not mentioned the Civil War or local politics at all - these belong in other books; but I hope I have indicated that the town seen in the Frith views has much of its earlier framework or skeleton intact, with Georgian and Victorian facades jostling with or concealing Tudor or earlier timber-framed houses. This was a working town that grew up, like Marlow, fed by the river trade that transported the goods and produce of the hinterland, mainly to London. It had small houses too, and Friday Street was where the poorer tradesmen and labourers lived.

However, by 1847 James Thorn could write in 'Rambles by Rivers' that 'there are several large inns, to which was formerly a considerable posting trade attached, but it was almost destroyed by the railway'. The railway had, of course, missed the town, which was hardly surprising given its hilly surroundings. This decline after the railway had destroyed its river trade as well as the coaching trade led the town to look elsewhere for survival.

When a branch line finally arrived in 1857, Henley developed both as a commuter town and as a leisure one. Henley was ahead in that game - its Regatta was a master-stroke, for it was founded by the citizens well before the great late Victorian and Edwardian boating boom; a boom depicted so wonderfully in Jerome K Jerome's 'Three Men in a Boat' published in 1889. Henley had latched on to the newly-fashionable sport of rowing; this preceded the later Victorian boom, which also enthused the lower middle classes with their increased leisure and spending money. Its first coup was the very first Oxford and Cambridge boat race, held at Henley in 1829. Thus a river port with the piles of grain along its wharves, depicted in Ward's 1835 painting 'A View of Henley Bridge', was transformed by the fashionable rowing fraternity and by an event that became a key event in the social calendar: the Henley Royal Regatta. Leisure, tourism and shopping replaced commerce, and the town revived; the railway station serviced the Regatta and that new phenomenon, the middle class commuter who travelled daily to London.

The 1890s: Emily Climenson's Henley

Market Place 1893 31732

In 1896 Mrs Emily J Climenson published 'A Guide to Henley on Thames'. This remarkable and invaluable picture of the town and its surroundings was written just as Frith's photographers made their first major visit to the town, partly to record the Regattas and partly the town and river. If we combine Emily Climenson's 'Guide' and Frith's photographs with information from G R Smith's 'Postal Directory of Reading and Neighbourhood' of 1894, a picture of the town at the end of the Victorian era can be brought vividly to life.

The 'Guide' appeared at an opportune moment in the town's history; for after over seven hundred and fifty years of existence as a town, Henley had at last received borough status in 1883 (under the cumbersomely-named Municipal Corporation New Charter Act of 1877). The old town corporation of the mayor, two bridgemen, ten aldermen and sixteen burgesses was replaced by a mayor, four aldermen and twelve councillors. Henley's Town Clerks demonstrate the remarkable continuity so often seen in provincial towns: five generations of the Cooper family, solicitors in West Street, held the post in succession from 1777 until 1914.

The new borough council continued to meet in the Town Hall built by Alderman Burgess in 1795; the foundation stone had been laid that June by Mayor Robert Brakspear, the brewer. It was a rather provincial classical building with an open ground floor like that at High Wycombe, but this was later filled in. The year after Emily

Climenson published her 'Guide', the council decided that a better Town Hall was needed, so the old one was demolished to make way for the present one. The foundation stone was laid on 9 June 1899, and it was completed and opened in March 1901. The new council and its Town Hall can be seen as symbolic of the confidence and prosperity of the town by the end of the 19th century: it had fully recovered from the doldrums of the 1830s to the 1850s.

There had been many changes, of course, that produced the 1890s town, whose centre is remarkably little changed today. The demolishing of the 1795 Town Hall put the finishing touches to a process of clearing away market place encroachment that had resulted in buildings, shops, stalls and houses being erected all the way up the centre of Market Place and the west half of Hart Street. Middle Row, Butcher's Row and Fisher's Row were cleared in the later 18th century, along with the old Guildhall; it had stood near the Bell Street and Duke Street cross-roads, and apparently fell down in 1760.

In the newly-liberated space the corporation erected a tall and elegant stone obelisk in the 1780s, the first attempt to give the space civic dignity in the approved Palladian and Classical way. It served as a milestone, and had a water pump attached, which was used for washing the streets after market day. Its use for street washing was stopped about 1797; it remained as a signpost until 1885, when it was moved to Northfield End, as we see in view 43014, pages 32-33.

Its place was taken by a highly ornate Gothic-style water fountain, its pinnacles encrusted with stone crockets and surmounted by a stone cross. The fountain, erected in memory of Greville Phillimore, the rector from 1867 to 1883, was in the correct Victorian public works style, and was a marked contrast to the beautifully-proportioned and simple Classical obelisk. Its reign at this prominent cross-roads was all too brief: in 1903, soon after the view on this page was taken, it was moved to its present location by the church. Its predecessor, the obelisk itself, survived at Northfield End until 1970. It has now been re-erected in Millmarsh Meadows park and, as a plaque informs us, 'it now serves as a link with the past'.

The prosperity of the town was reflected in some rebuilding in the centre, with something of a bias towards timber-framed gables and Arts and Crafts forms, together with typical Victorian cavalier disregard for the scale of surrounding older buildings; medieval and Tudor styles were more in favour than Georgian ones. The Westminster Bank in the Market Place, now the NatWest, was built in 1897, presumably to rival the enormous and gross London and County Bank in Hart Street - this was built in 1892 and is now Barclays Bank.

Another example, opposite the station, is the Imperial Hotel: it was built in 1897, and has three storeys over a basement, with further rooms within the enormous gable. It is decked with timber-framing, bay windows, and balconies, all over-scaled compared with the Tudor work they aped. Indeed, much Victorian development had taken place to the west of the old town centre. Stimulated by the arrival of the railway in 1857, the population was climbing: the 1891 Census recorded it as 4,913, quite an increase from the 3,509 population recorded in Pigot's Directory, which gave the 1821 figure.

Smith's Postal Directory of 1894 gives an interesting picture of the town, listing its tradesmen and market days. These included an annual horse fair on 7 March; the corn and general markets were on Thursdays. Another important market and fair was one in early September for cheese, pleasure (a fun fair) and for the hiring of servants, both domestic and agricultural.

The pleasure fair had moved its temporary booths and stalls from Market Place by 1896, but Mrs Climenson quotes a Mr Richardson's poem 'Henley' which describes the hiring fair earlier in the 19th century. At that time, each tradesman or labourer wore tokens of his trade as he waited to catch the eye of a future employer:

'The carter's hat coarse whip-cords now adorn,
The thresher bears a sheaf of ripened corn,
With hair of kine the herdsman is o'erspread,
And fleecy honours deck the shepherd's head.'

However, she adds that 'these emblems have now disappeared in favour of streamers of ribbon'.

Emily Climenson gives a wonderfully evocative view of the town, as well as sections on its history and places to visit in the area - these include Fawley Court, Greys Court and Park Place. She rounds her guide off with a delightfully earnest chapter on the local geology, along with an astonishingly long list of the

MARKET PLACE c1900 H73505

flora found in the Henley area. Within the book are chapters on 'Public Buildings, etc', and 'Trade, Amusements, etc'. These are the sections that paint a fascinating picture of life in a provincial town in the 1890s, and of the remarkable range of clubs, pubs and facilities one could find in those days.

The list of clubs and societies includes the Druids Lodge, the 'Royal Jubilee' Lodge, which was founded in 1887, the year of Queen Victoria's Golden Jubilee, and then had over 150 members (all men of course), the Ancient Order of Odd Fellows, with over 250 members, and a 'flourishing tent' of the Independent Order of Rechabites, which had three 'tents' - men, women and juveniles - with a total of 233 members. Rechabites were total abstainers from the demon drink; there was also a flourishing Total Abstinence Society in the town, which had been founded in 1859, but Mrs Climenson does not give the number of members. My eye was caught by the curiously-named Pleasant Sunday Afternoon Society with 130 members. This was a non-sectarian group of church people dedicated to 'get if possible the men who never attended any church' by enticing them with string bands to accompany hymns and solos by members, teas and good speakers.

Under amusements Mrs Climenson lists and gives thumb-nail sketches of numerous more frivolous organisations, including Henley Cycling Club and Henley Wheelers Cycling Club; the latter was aimed at young working men. There were also sports

The 1890s: Emily Climenson's Henley

Details From: The Market Place c1900 H73505 & Market Place 1893 31732

The two previous views were taken looking to and from the Town Hall at the west end of the Market Place. The Town Hall in 31732 was the one that was built in 1796, replacing one that had fallen down near the cross-roads in 1760, and was itself replaced in 1899-1901. The portico and various parts were re-erected as part of a house at Crazies Hill, near Wargrave on the Berkshire side of the river, by a Mr Charles Clements. The Gothic drinking fountain was installed in 1885 as a memorial to Greville Phillimore, Rector of Henley 1867-1883; it replaced a 1780s stone obelisk. The drinking fountain was in its turn removed to a location near the church in 1903.

clubs for football, cricket, lawn tennis and swimming. Of course the Royal Regatta has a long entry in this section, though I suspect a few eyebrows were raised at including this deadly serious business in an amusement section.

The 'Guide' has a section describing the virtues of the various breweries, including Brakspears, of course, in New Street, Greys in Friday Street, and Ive Brothers in Market Place; the last two are no longer in existence. Mrs Climenson then says: 'Having exhausted beer, we must turn to boats'. She must have been quite a character! She then describes the various boathouses and boat companies, and the hirers of electric launches. Hobbs and Sons are still in successful business in Henley.

EXTRACT FROM BARBER'S GAZETTEER OF ENGLAND & WALES 1895

A weekly market is held on Thursday, and fairs are held on 7 March, Holy Thursday, and the Thursday after Trinity Sunday. There is also a statute hiring fair on the Thursday after 21 September.

However, we must return to the not-yet-exhausted beer, for Brakspear's Henley Brewery is still within the town, brewing real ale in New Street. They have survived; but Greys went out of business in 1896, at about the time Mrs Climenson's 'Guide' was published. With the temperance movement so strong in the late Victorian period, many breweries went under. Henley, as we have seen earlier, had two flourishing total abstinence societies and the consequent reduction in local consumption was a direct cause of Greys' demise.

Now, however, the town is proud of its brewery, and most guides recount the story of Robert Brakspear, the nephew of Richard Hayward, who brewed and malted in Henley. In 1775 Robert, the son of a Faringdon tailor, and by nineteen the landlord of a coaching inn at Witney, came to join his uncle, who had bought a number of local inns as his business expanded. In 1779 Brakspear's was founded. Robert became a prominent citizen: he was the mayor who laid the foundation stone for the 1795 Town Hall.

Robert's second son William took over in 1812 upon Robert's death. William became a partner in 1825, and ran the business successfully until his death in 1882. A plaque in the church tells us that Robert's widow died in 1863 aged 99, after half a century of widowhood. 'To this present Messrs Archibald, George Brakspear and Sons succeeded'; Emily Climenson gives the then hot news that 'in the early part of 1896 the firm was formed into a limited company'. She adds: 'the quaint old yard doorway is decorated every Christmas morning with a huge bush of holly and mistletoe, which remains hung up till the ensuing Christmas morning, when a new bush takes its place'. There was much building in the 1890s. This included the former Mineral Water Manufactory, which was, no doubt, an attempt to diversify into supplying the towns' numerous total abstainers with refreshment, and the maltings on the north side of New Street in 1899; this had two tall ventilation towers, a rival in river views to the parish church tower.

Emily Climenson's fourth chapter, 'Public Buildings, etc', is much more than that: it informs us that in January 1896 the Corporation was presented with 'handsome robes of office, of crimson cloth trimmed with sable fur' by Mr Gardner of Joyce Grove, Nettlebed. There is a vast amount of information in this chapter on the postal services, including the observation that the new post office in Reading Road, which opened in June 1895, caused 'much regret ... at the new buildings not being built on the site or near the old office in the Market Place, a more central situation, with easier access. However, the new buildings are handsome and commodious'. There is a section on the bridge, the Town Hall, and the 'Smith' Isolation Hospital founded in 1892 by WH Smith, the newsagent, who lived at Greenlands, up river near Hambleden. There was a volunteer fire brigade, a gas works which 'date from the year 1834', and the Union, or workhouse, built in 1790 with accommodation for 263 inmates, mostly the elderly poor of a pre-Welfare State era.

A Conservative Club was founded in 1886, and its 'handsome and convenient' building in Queen Street opened in 1894. The Liberal Club, not to be outdone, also opened in 1894 in the Market Place. Mrs Climenson says that it has 'three large rooms, consisting of a reading-room, smoking- and game-room, and a billiard-room fitted with one of Burroughs and Watts' latest tables'. She then lists the hotels and inns, with the Red Lion receiving the longest

THE 1890S: EMILY CLIMENSON'S HENLEY

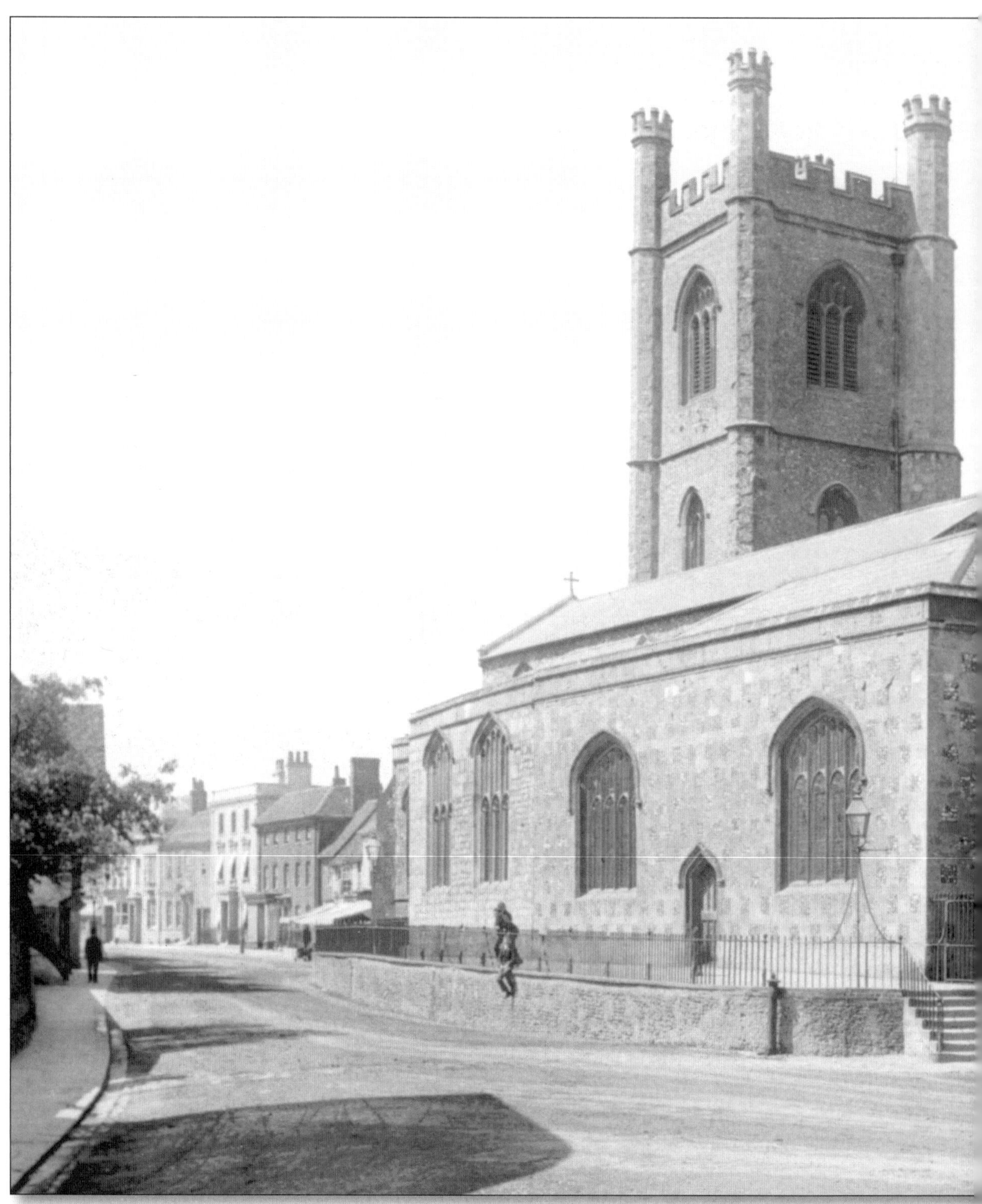

HART STREET AND THE CHURCH

This photograph shows the Red Lion, a former coaching inn largely rebuilt in the early 18th century; the porch was added in 1889 when the central carriageway was infilled to provide the hotel's reception hall.

THE CHURCH AND THE RED LION HOTEL 1893 31734

entry; this is partly because all sorts of illustrious guests stayed there, ranging from King Charles I to Dr Johnson and Boswell. Many of the inns and hotels are noted as having Burroughs and Watts billiard tables - perhaps Emily Climenson was a keen player. The Oxford Temperance Hotel charged one shilling a night for a bed, with hot dinners from eightpence halfpenny upwards. She lists doctors or 'Medical Men'; then there is a long section on churches. Mrs Climenson informs us that the rectory on Waterside, a fine Georgian house near the Angel and now offices, was bought for £1999 in 1830 by the then rector.

As one might expect, there were numerous churches and chapels in the town in the 1890s, ranging from Wesleyan, Friends, and Strict Baptists to Roman Catholics. There was a Masonic Lodge, whose Tudor-style building in Reading Street was built in 1890. The chapter is rounded off by two volunteer units: the Queen's Own Oxfordshire Hussars (Yeomanry), with drill, etc, in the Queen's Hall, and the Henley Volunteers, Company D of the Oxfordshire Light Infantry, whose headquarters was the Town Hall - but they were socially a cut below the Hussars, of course. Apparently a 'Morris Tube Range was opened in January 1896, erected at the back of the Bull Inn, Bell Street' for the Volunteers, presumably a rifle range of some sort.

THE 1890S: EMILY CLIMENSON'S HENLEY

Left: HART STREET 1893 31733

This 1893 view of the Catherine Wheel, an inn by 1499, shows it just before it took over the two Georgian brick houses beyond. On the right, the street still awaits the out-of-scale London and Counties bank, erected in 1892. The optician on the right is still an optician.

THE BRIDGE AND THE RIVERSIDE

These two views both feature the fine Georgian river bridge and the southern part of Riverside, sometimes called Thames Side; by this date it was solely used for mooring and hiring pleasure craft, not for corn barges. Both views show the Angel Hotel by the bridge and the Rectory to its left - one shows a top-hatted coachman driving past. This house with its early 18th-century front was bought by the then rector, James King, and given 'in perpetuity' as a residence for the rectors of Henley. His wishes were not respected - this fine building is now used as offices.

Below: THE BRIDGE & THE VICARAGE 1893 31729

Below Left: THE BRIDGE 1893 31730

7

ESTABLISHED 1849.

DREWETT'S

ROYAL CARRIAGE MANUFACTORY

Northfield End,

HENLEY-ON-THAMES.

Coach Builder to Her Royal Highness Princess Louise, Marquis of Lorne, German Ambassador, Henman Hatzfeldt and German Embassy, &c.

GEO. TURTON GREEN,

(Late BATCHELOR),

Dispensing & Family Chemist

41, BELL STREET,

Henley-on-Thames.

Physicians' Prescriptions accurately dispensed. Family Recipes carefully prepared. Pure Drugs and Chemicals. Toilet Requisites and Proprietary Articles. Patent Medicines and Photographic Sundries.

Emily Climenson's 'Guide' finishes with pages of local advertisements for Henley businesses and trades, ranging from Brakspear's and its Celebrated Henley Ales to Drewett's Royal Carriage Manufactory at Northfield End and McBean Brothers, the ironmongers, in Hart Street; their advertisement illustrates a cumbersome patent lawn mower. Simmons and Sons, the land agents, valuers and auctioneers, who also had an advertisement, are still in the town; they were established in 1846. Thus in the 1890s, when the Frith photographers made their first major sally into Henley, the town was possessed of a rich range of facilities that you could not match in the modern town; the 'Guide' gives a splendid snapshot of the town just at that time.

NORTHFIELD END

Northfield End is a northward expansion of the town. It has some good Georgian houses, such as Countess Gardens, which we can see here in the distance beyond the bracket clock. The stone obelisk with bracket lamps was erected in the Market Place in the 1780s; it was removed in 1885, and re-erected here in Northfield End in 1886. This view is taken from the Nettlebed road at the start of the Fair Mile - the Marlow road is on the left. The Pack Horse pub closed in 1964 and is now a private house. The bracket clock belongs to Drewett's the coach builders, coach builders by appointment to royalty and the nobility, established in 1849.

OXFORD ROAD AND THE OBELISK 1899 43014

HENLEY-ON-THAMES FROM THE AIR 1935 AFR867

THE RIVER BRIDGE & THE RIVER SIDE

THE RIVER BRIDGE

The c1870, pages 38-39, view is the oldest Frith view in the book, and shows the bridge when it was still a toll bridge. In 1873 the £10,000 debt for its building was paid off, and with great local rejoicing the tollgate was removed. The tollkeeper's cottage on the left was later demolished as well. The Leander Rowing Clubhouse was built in the 1890s in the field to the left: there has been much change here since 1870. This view shows all five arches of the bridge, the central keystone carved with the head of Isis.

The River Bridge & the River Side

The Bridge c1960 H73056

The River Bridge & the River Side

Henley's bridge over the River Thames has been central to the entire history of the town, and the present Georgian one is rightly the focus of Henley's riverside. It replaced the timber bridge which had been swept away in March 1774; this had been closed since 1754 owing to its dangerous condition, and had been replaced by a ferry. The destroyed medieval bridge had lasted a considerable time. It suffered serious damage in 1642 during the Civil War; repairs were reluctantly carried out in 1670, but as was often the case with any needed expenditure on public buildings and works, the 18th century was an era of penny-pinching false economy. This neglect was, as it happens, a good thing for us, as the new bridge is a most elegant and graceful one with its five arches and balustraded parapets.

Before looking at the Georgian bridge, let us look briefly at what is known of the earlier one. It was first built in about 1170, judging by the stone arches found on the Berkshire bank in 1984 during excavations on the site of the present Henley Royal Regatta building. After this, divers found evidence for medieval stone piers in the main river bed, so perhaps the medieval bridge had been entirely of stone; this was certainly the opinion of John Leland. There is another bridge arch surviving on the Henley side, which is now in the cellars of the Angel. In 1223 timber was granted from the Royal Forest of Windsor for bridge works, and indulgences were granted in 1230 to those who contributed to the bridge.

Perhaps the main part of the bridge was reconstructed in timber or stone in the 1220s. There are subsequent mentions of various donations towards bridge repair in medieval deeds and wills, as well as references to a chapel, St Anne's, which was actually built on the bridge. In 1483 the bridge was certainly rebuilt in timber after furious storms. Soon after this, the veil of history was lifted by John Leland's 'Itinerary', written in the 1540s. He wrote: 'the bridge is all of tymbre, as moste parte of the bridgs be ther about. It was of stone, as the foundation shewith at low water'. This description is over a century and a half before the famous 1690 paintings by Jan Siberechts, which do indeed show a timber bridge with two stone arches at the Berkshire end and one at the Henley end.

The storms of March 1774 brought prodigious floods: there is a mark on the wall of the Red Lion which shows how high the waters reached. The rickety timber bridge, closed for twenty years, was

no match for the surging waters, and it disappeared downstream. In those days, events moved rather more slowly than the storm-filled river; it was not until 1781 that an Act of Parliament was secured for a rebuilding. The economically hard-pressed town had to accept the demolition of some houses, the removal of part of the churchyard and the demolition of the Almshouses founded in 1547 by Bishop Longland to give a wider access to the bridge - the existing lane was narrow, steep and dangerous.

The Bridge Commissioners dealt with all this, and eventually

THE RIVER BRIDGE & THE RIVER SIDE

THE BRIDGE c1870 H73501

the architect, William Hayward from Shropshire, was appointed. He was known locally: he had been assistant to John Gwynn, who designed Magdalen Bridge in Oxford. Unfortunately, he died of a chill contracted by 'voluntarily resigning his seat within [the coach] to accommodate a woman who was suffering from her exposed situation without [that is on the outside seats of the coach]'. This was in 1782; he died before the bridge had advanced very far in its construction, if at all. He is buried in the churchyard, and has a monument in the church tower.

The bridge progressed, though Mrs Anne Damer commented on the lounging drunkenness of the workmen. She was the daughter of Field Marshal Conway, the owner of Park Place on the Berkshire side, and a great builder and beautifier of his house and landscaped grounds. Both were friends of Horace Walpole; indeed, Walpole left his Gothic extravaganza of a mansion at Strawberry Hill, near Twickenham, to Mrs Damer. She was a noted sculptor, and was awarded the task of carving the keystones for the central arch of the bridge. The personifications of the river, Thame and Isis, were chosen as the subjects, Thame on the keystone facing downstream and Isis facing upstream towards Oxford - Isis is the name by which the Thames was known above Dorchester.

The keystones clearly impressed Walpole, and confirmed his deep admiration for Mrs Damer: 'the masks of the Thame and Isis ... are among those Works which have amused a mind capable of blending the exertions of Genius and the attractions of female Grace and the charm of polished Life'. (Walpole also enthused effusively over the new bridge when it was completed). Thame is represented by Mrs Damer as a bearded man with bullrushes in his hair and fish in his beard, while Isis is female with water plants in her hair. The mask keystones are impressive, but not perhaps as great as the admiring Horace Walpole said they were.

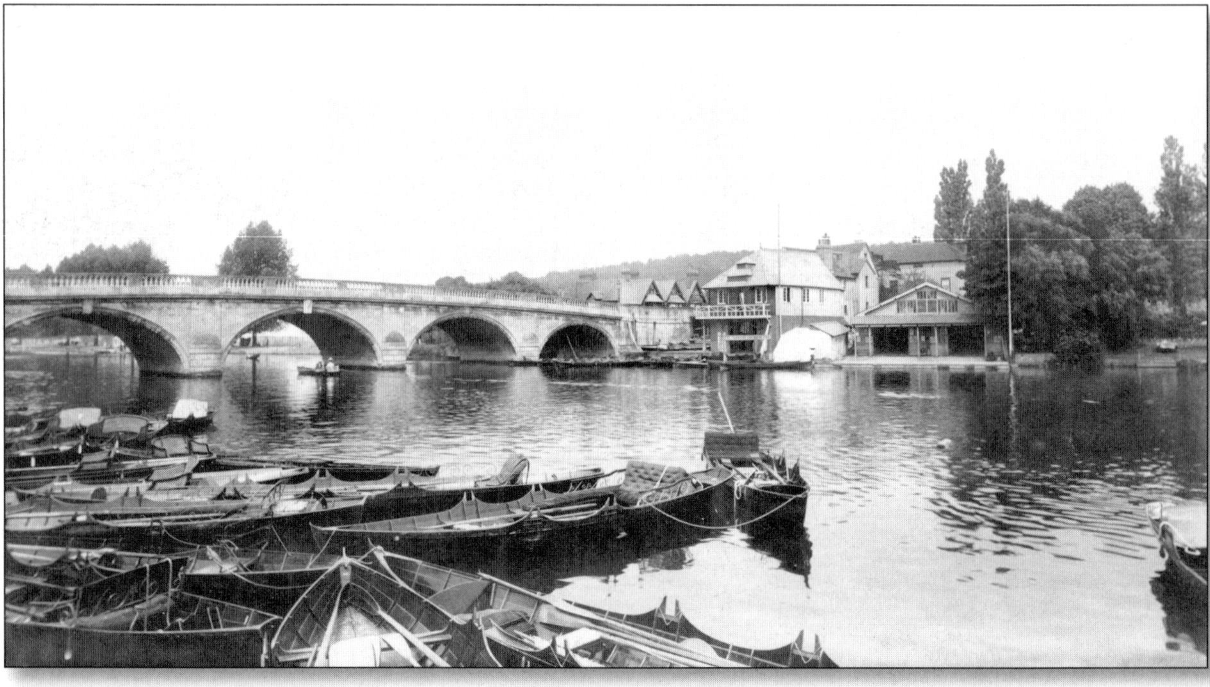

The River Bridge & the River Side

THE EAST AND WEST ENDS OF THE BRIDGE

These views show each end of the bridge - two were taken in 1890. Photograph looks from the Berkshire side, from the balcony of the Carpenter's Arms landing stage towards its rival, The Angel, whose tall 18th-century bay-windowed river elevation and riverside terrace are a well-known and very popular landmark; the Angel is perhaps the most photographed building in Henley. The other two views show the Carpenters Arms landing stage and boathouse, which in 1955 were rented to J G Meakes Ltd. The Carpenters Arms inn was built in 1714, but it was demolished in 1984 to make way for the Henley Royal Regatta headquarters.

Left: THE BRIDGE 1890 27191

Bottom Left: THE BRIDGE 1890 27196

Below: THE BRIDGE c1955 H73043

The River Bridge & the River Side

Right: The View from The Red Lion Hotel Gardens 1893 31736

Below: The Leander Club House 1899 43011

Bottom: The New Boathouses 1893 31731

The River Bridge & the River Side

THE LEANDER CLUB ARRIVES

The Leander Rowing Club, the most exclusive and oldest rowing club in the world, was founded around 1818 in London; it had a clubhouse in Putney, built in 1866. In the early 1890s Henley town council offered the club a lease on the Nook Enclosure on the Berkshire bank near the bridge at £25 per annum rent, on condition that their clubhouse, later nicknamed the Pink Palace, was finished by 24 June 1898. This view shows Nook Meadow, with the house that replaced the old bridge tollkeeper's cottage on the right, and 43011 on the left shows the new Leander clubhouse.

The bridge was finally completed in 1786, having cost £10,000. It was well-built, for it now has to withstand all the near-continuous and heavy traffic that the modern age can throw at it. For nearly a hundred years there was a toll gate across the bridge - the toll fees were used to cover the costs of building the bridge. The tolls ranged from 1d for a horse to 10d per twenty cattle, 5d per twenty sheep or 3d per carriage horse. That last toll would mean that a four-in-hand coach would cost one shilling to cross. A tollkeeper's cottage, an octagonal building with a central chimney, was built on the Berkshire bank where the gate was situated. It was not until 1873 that the costs of the bridge were finally paid off. The 1870 photograph (see H73501) in this chapter shows the tollgate and cottage in its last years. The cottage itself was demolished in the 1880s, but the tollgate was removed to local enthusiasm in 1873.

The River Bridge & the River Side

Right: The Riverside c1955 H73029

Below Right: Tow Path Scene c1955 H73032

RIVERSIDE NORTH OF THE BRIDGE

These views span from the 1890s to the 1960s, and take us north along the river as far as Temple Island, the Regatta starting point. The 1893 view towards the bridge (page 42) is little changed, with only the c1900 Little White Hart hotel replacing some cottages. The premises of Shepherd & Dee, the boatbuilders, are now two art galleries. Behind are the church tower and the chimneys of Brakspear's Brewery. Other views show the malting oast towers of 1899 and the late 1880s boathouses of Hobbs and Sons, with their gables and balconies. One 1955 view, H73009 page 47, shows camping punts for hire.

EXTRACT FROM BARBER'S GAZETTEER OF ENGLAND & WALES 1895

A fine stone bridge of five arches connects it with Berks, was erected in 1768, in place of an old wooden one, at a cost of £10,000, and has sculptures over the central arch representing by ideal heads the rivers Thames and Isis, which were executed by the Hon Mrs Damer.

The 1870 view of the bridge is particularly interesting, for it shows the Berkshire bank before the spread of late Victorian developments that brought large houses and villas to the Berkshire hillside, and of course, before the Leander Clubhouse by the river, the 'Pink Palace', was built. We can see the Carpenters Arms pub and Thames House behind it on the right; the former was demolished to make way for the present Henley Royal Regatta headquarters building, an exciting design by Terry Farrell, which opened in 1986.

The Leander Rowing Club had its origins in 1818 further downstream in Putney, where the early 19th-century sporting fraternity gambled on teams of oarsmen. It is regarded as the oldest rowing club in the world, and has an exclusive membership of exceptional oarsmen, past and present. Leander took part in the regatta from 1840 on, winning very frequently indeed; from 1890 it had an enclosure on Temple Island, at the Regatta start. The town council then offered the club a lease on the Nook Enclosure on the Berkshire bank near the bridge at £25 per annum rent, on condition that their clubhouse was built and occupied by 24 June 1898. The clubhouse, which also had bedrooms, was completed before that date. It was soon nicknamed the 'Pink Palace', and has been an important riverside feature ever since.

The River Bridge & the River Side

Right: Temple Island 1899 43013

Below Left: The Reach 1890 27197

Below Far Left: A Riverside Scene c1955 H73009

From the river bank near the Leander Club we can look across to the river front of Henley and imagine its bankside wharfs alive with the shouts of bargees and watermen loading their barges, with great mounds of corn, stacks of timber and other produce on the quayside. The front was a mix of warehouses and inns to slake the prodigious thirsts of the wharfingers, but during the 19th century things changed.

By the 1890s the leisure boathouses and boat builders had taken over, interspersed with inns and hotels catering for the visitors who flocked to the river in and out of the Regatta season. From the bridge northwards, first was the Red Lion, once a great coaching inn which adapted to the changing times by rebuilding most of its stable block as boathouses in 1888 - the stable blocks themselves had replaced warehouses in the 18th century. These are now the Century and Wyfold Galleries, but for years they were the premises of Shepherd and Dee, boat builders. Tom Shepherd was also proprietor of the Red Lion itself; he was a Victorian entrepreneur, and saw the possibilities of diversifying beyond pulling pints.

Next along were a range of old cottages, which were replaced around 1900 by the Little White Hart Hotel. Then comes a pub, the Cottage Inn, and the boathouse of the Henley Rowing Club, established in 1839, who took over an old warehouse in 1903; they moved to the Berkshire side south of the bridge in 1986. Behind loomed the chimneys and brew tower of Brakspear's brewery. Beyond New Street, Hobbs and Sons built their range of five-gabled boathouses with upper floor balconies, which became prime sites for viewing the Regatta. The company was established in 1870, and it has boathouses and works to the south of the bridge too, as well as modern yards on the Berkshire bank. Beyond are two more boathouse/houses, Waters Edge and Wharfe Boathouse. All these replaced timber wharves and warehouses, as we can see in the 1890 view of the Reach looking towards Temple Island. Behind on the east side of New Street were Brakspear's maltings, built in 1899. These can all be seen in the riverside panorama on pages 42-43.

South of the bridge, we have the Angel Inn, built in the 18th

CAMPING PUNTS
FOR HIRE

THE RIVER BRIDGE & THE RIVER SIDE

RIVERSIDE SOUTH OF THE BRIDGE

These views take us downstream towards the bridge from the south. We start in Marshmill Meadows park, and then go past Hobbs and Sons' southern boatyard and chandlery, with the Salter's Steamers 'Goring' taking on 1950s passengers, and Royal Mansions, once an hotel. Then comes Riverside, (H73024, pages 50-51) the tall stucco mid-19th century terrace. Along past the Friday Street junction is Arlett's launch hire office by the river, (H73006, pages 52-53) a 1950 building, now Alf Parrott Moorings Ltd. Beyond is the Old Rectory, now offices, a good early 18th-century brick-fronted building.

Left: THE PROMENADE c1965 H73082

Below: A PLEASURE STEAMER ON THE THAMES c1955 H73013

century, with its cellars under the old bridge's stone arch. Along Riverside, housing for the gentry, including the Old Rectory, with its fine early 18th-century brick refronting, soon gives way to warehouses and the workaday side of the town's pre-Victorian economy. Then comes the old timber-framed warehouses, now a house, The Old Granary, at the corner of Friday Street. The south side of Friday Street was outside the town boundary until 1892; it was within Rotherfield Greys parish, and so beyond the reach of the market and trade tolls imposed by the corporation on all commerce within its boundaries. Thus other trading houses and warehouses were built along this part of the riverside. Baltic Cottage, on the south corner of Friday Street, is a reminder of this period; it was the local headquarters of the Baltic Exchange trading organisation until the late 19th century.

South of the old core, there was gradual expansion. Beyond a stucco terrace of the 1850s is the former Royal Hotel of 1900, all timber-framed gables and balconies. This was the second hotel on the site; the earlier one was built in 1864 as a house, and was converted into an hotel in 1872. The Royal was converted into housing in 1925, and renamed Royal Mansions. Beyond Station Road is Hobbs and Sons' boathouse - river excursions have long departed from here. Westwards is the railway terminus, and southwards new housing, Boathouse Reach and then Millmarsh Meadows. Henley certainly addresses the river far more than Wallingford or Marlow do, for example. This gives the town a different character - the town's structure is far more visible from and related to the river.

FROM THE TOWPATH c1955 H73024

The River Bridge & the River Side

RIVERSIDE c1955 H73006

HOUSEBOATS 1899 43012

THE RIVER SOUTH OF HENLEY

This photograph was taken looking south towards Marsh Mills and Marsh Lock. Flag-bedecked houseboats are moored for Regatta Week in 1899. We can see Marsh Weir in the distance, and the wooded hills on the left are part of the grounds of Park Place.

Oxfordshire County Map

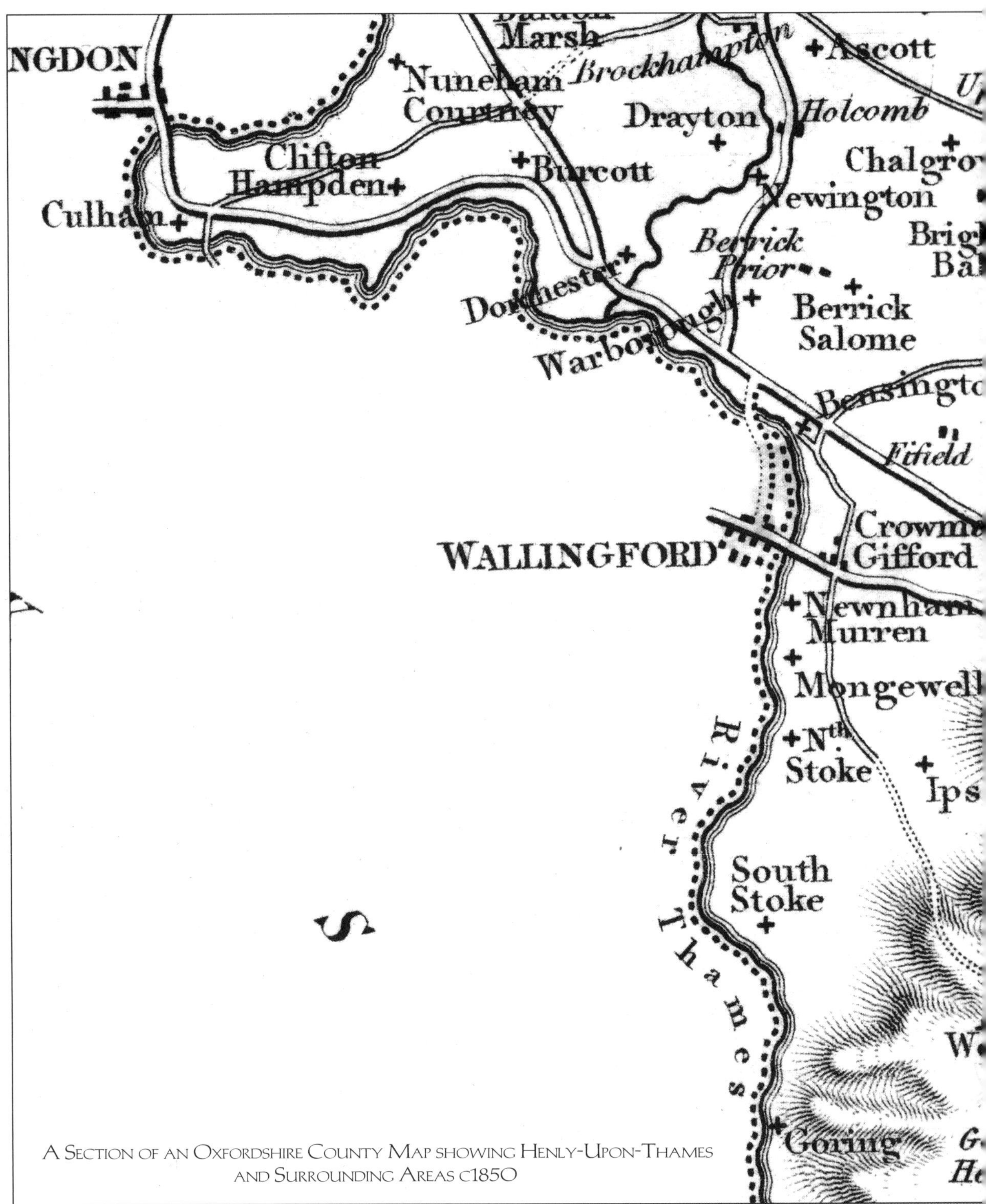

A Section of an Oxfordshire County Map showing Henly-Upon-Thames and Surrounding Areas c1850

Sth. Weston
Lewknor
Stoken Church
Shirburn
Pirton
WATLINGTON
to High Wycombe
Brightwell Salome
Brightwell Prior
Ipstone
Swincomb
Ackhamstead
Cookley Green
Pishill
Bix
Nettlebed
To Grt Marlow
Assington Cross
HENLEY upon Thames
Rotherfield Grays
Rotherfield Peppard
Harpsden
Kidmoor
Bolney

A View of the Town in the 1950s & 1960s

Physically, much of the town recorded by the Frith photographers in the 1950s and 1960s looks relatively little changed from that shown in the earlier photographers' 1890s visits. However, this similarity is in some ways skin deep: many of the town centre houses had become offices, and many of the individual shops had become branches of chain stores, chain chemists and the like. The town had also expanded greatly. Almost all the expansion was to the south; growth in other directions was constrained by private parks and the River Thames. The population of Emily Climenson's Henley had thus grown from 4,913 in 1891 to over ten thousand by the 1980s, with numerous housing estates providing homes for thousands of new citizens.

By the 1960s the tourist side of the town was well reflected in the numerous tea rooms and restaurants, not to mention the pubs and hotels. Antique shops and art galleries have also sprung up, and so have high-class dress shops. These are individual businesses; but the supply of most other things, from aspirin to bread to newspapers and magazines, seems to be in the hands of chain stores. The long-term impact of Waitrose and Tesco will probably be an increase in the number of antique shops, clothes shops and galleries in the town centre at the expense of food and produce shops, with the exception of delicatessens and speciality food shops.

This is not peculiar to Henley, of course: Marlow or Wallingford, two similar-sized towns in the area, have experienced the same changes. Estate agents seem to remain in large numbers - there were plenty in the 1890s views as well. Pubs and inns are prevalent too, though they are not nearly as numerous as in earlier years: in the late 19th century there were over sixty pubs and inns, while now there are only about thirty. This still respectable number is a reflection of Henley's tourism role nowadays; in earlier times, the prodigious thirst of the wharfingers and bargees was enough explanation.

However, amid all this change virtually no business listed in the 1894 directory or advertised at the back of Emily Climenson's 1896 'Guide' survives. Superficially, Gabriel Machin's butcher's shop founded in the 1880s on the south side of the Market Place still carries on; but in fact only the name does, for it is now run by the Marrett family, who retain the delightfully period-flavour name. The shop is now a speciality butcher and fishmonger. Another couple of examples of continuity are Frost, Borneo and Gregg, the opticians on the south side of Hart Street, which was established in 1860 as an optician and jeweller by the Barnard family, and the estate agents, valuers, auctioneers and surveyors Simmons and Sons, who were in the fine Georgian house nearby, No 18. They still exist in the town, but they have split into Simmons and Lawrence and Simmons and Son, both round the corner in Bell Street. However, No 18 is now the office of another estate agent, FDP Savills, so there is continuity there also. Further east, the Elizabethan House guest house and tea rooms is now a Caffe Uno.

The most evident continuities between 1890 and 1960 are the continued presence of Brakspear's Henley Brewery and Hobbs and Sons' boat business. The former has actually expanded, and

A View of the Town in the 1950s & 1960s

HART STREET: FROM THE ANGEL TO MARKET PLACE

In this set of four views (this page to page 63) of the bustling 1950s and 1960s town, superficially there is remarkably little change from the 1890s views in Emily Climenson's Henley. The main difference is the arrival of that great enemy of small towns, the motor car. The view of the Market Place shows the present proud Town Hall, opened in March 1901 and designed in Queen Anne style.

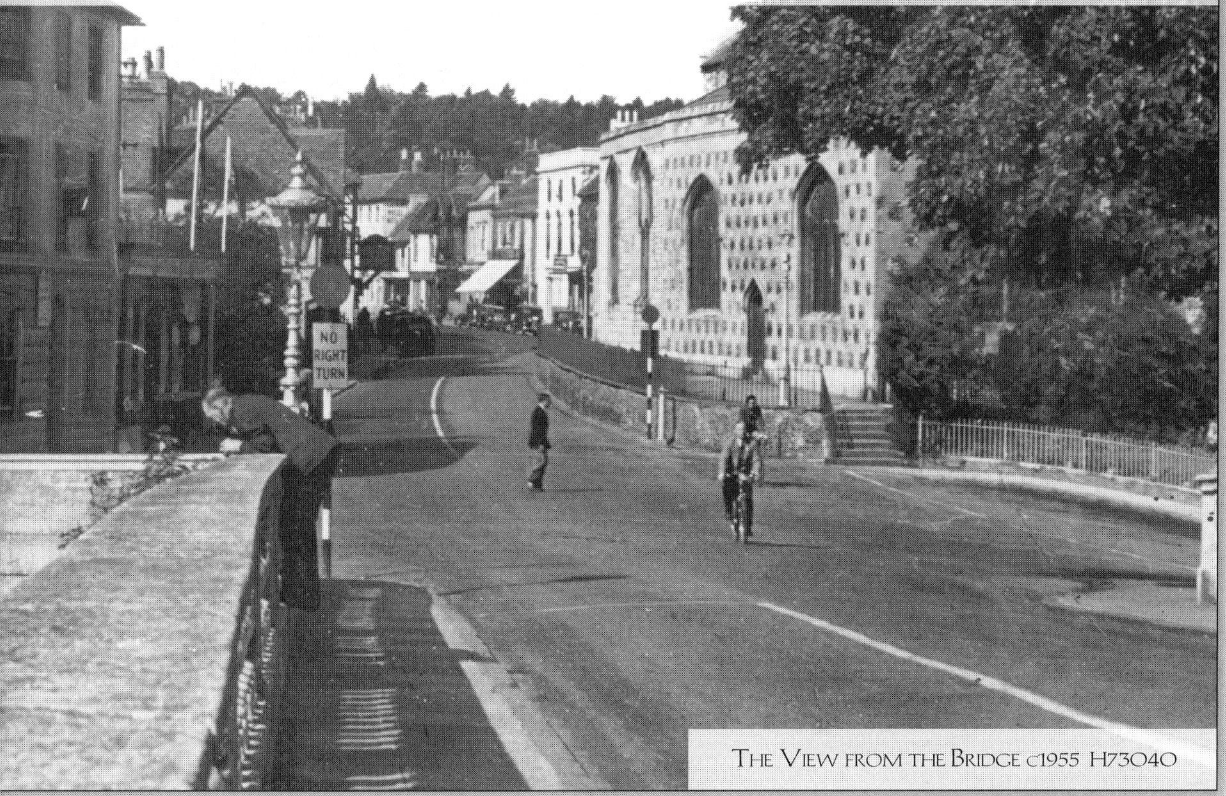

THE VIEW FROM THE BRIDGE c1955 H73040

has taken over several other buildings in its vicinity. Brakspear's weathered the Watneys Red revolution and gassy keg beers in the 1960s and 1970s to cash in on the 'real ale' phenomenon, and its tied houses are immensely popular venues for lunch in the Chiltern Hills as well as in town. However, this success also hides great changes and adaptations. For example, the vast maltings they built on the north side of New Street ceased malting in 1972. After a few years of being used for brewery storage they were converted into offices, and the two great oast towers were replaced by fibreglass replicas in the process.

Hobbs and Sons no longer own the boathouses at the end of New Street; they trade now from their boathouse, boat yard and chandlery on the south part of Riverside. They have also replaced their excursion steamers and launches by an imitation Mississippi stern wheeler with two tall smokestacks, the 'New Orleans'. Hobbs have a more modern premises and yard on the Berkshire bank as well.

Other changes have preserved the shells but not the substance. The old assembly rooms in Bell Street are now offices, for example, while the Palace Cinema in Bell Street, opened in 1911 in a converted 18th-century house, was replaced by the Regal Cinema in 1937. This was a typical Art Deco cum Modern Movement brick building; it looked totally out-of-place and out-of-scale amid Henley's domestic-scale streetscape, but its demolition in 1993 was vigorously contested both locally and nationally by cinema buffs. Its demolition was caused by the Waitrose development - this was equally controversial, but it has re-invigorated town centre shopping.

There have been numerous other changes, and also some rebuilding to replace ill-advised 1950s and 1960s buildings. An excellent example is at the corner of Market Place and Bell Street, where a rather fine stuccoed building, in the 1890s Monk's the drapers, founded in 1883, was demolished in the 1950s, along with No 4 Market Place; they were replaced by a gruesome single-storey Co-op. This went in the 1980s, and the present rendered neo-Georgian building on the corner is a great improvement. Opposite, on the Bell Street/Hart Street corner, Beningfield's premises was taken over in around 1910 by Timothy Whites Cash Chemist. In the 1960s it had its upper storey reduced in height for some reason; it is now Martin's the chain newsagents.

Notable in the Frith views of the 1950s and 1960s is the presence of the motor car, particularly cluttering up the Market Place and spoiling views of the Town Hall or down Hart Street. Since then, the traffic has increased greatly; various efforts at control have included the experimental pedestrianisation of the Market Place, which has since been eased, but the problem is one with which all popular towns have to cope. Marlow, further downstream, is also traffic-blighted, and it seems that there can never be enough spaces in the town's car parks. Through traffic is a distinct problem, and as for the Regatta, the queues of traffic are spectacular.

The town has many pubs and inns, but they are diminishing in numbers - some have been sold on or redeveloped as restaurants. For example, the White Hart is now an ASK pizza restaurant - and very well converted too. The Pack Horse at Northfield End is now a house, and so is the Basketmakers Arms on Gravel Hill. Other pubs and hotels are thriving, such as the Red Lion and the Catharine Wheel, while the Angel with its river terrace is always full.

TOWN HALL AND MARKET PLACE c1965 H73064

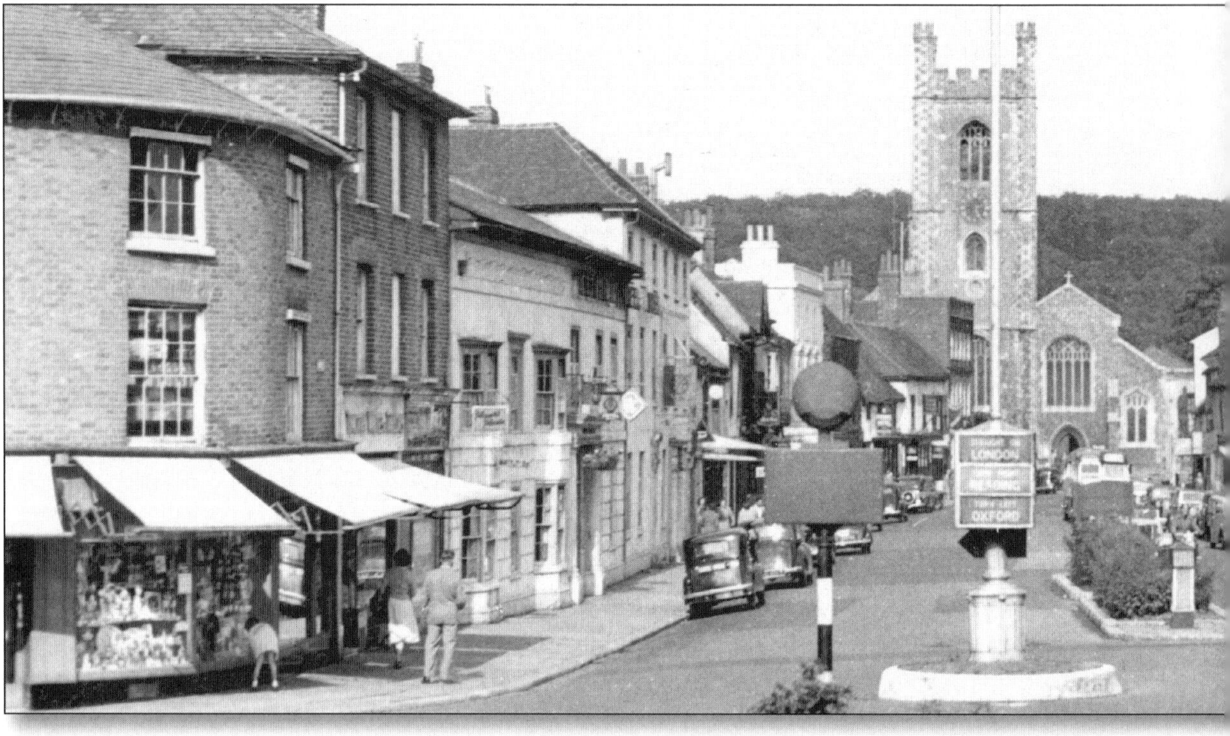

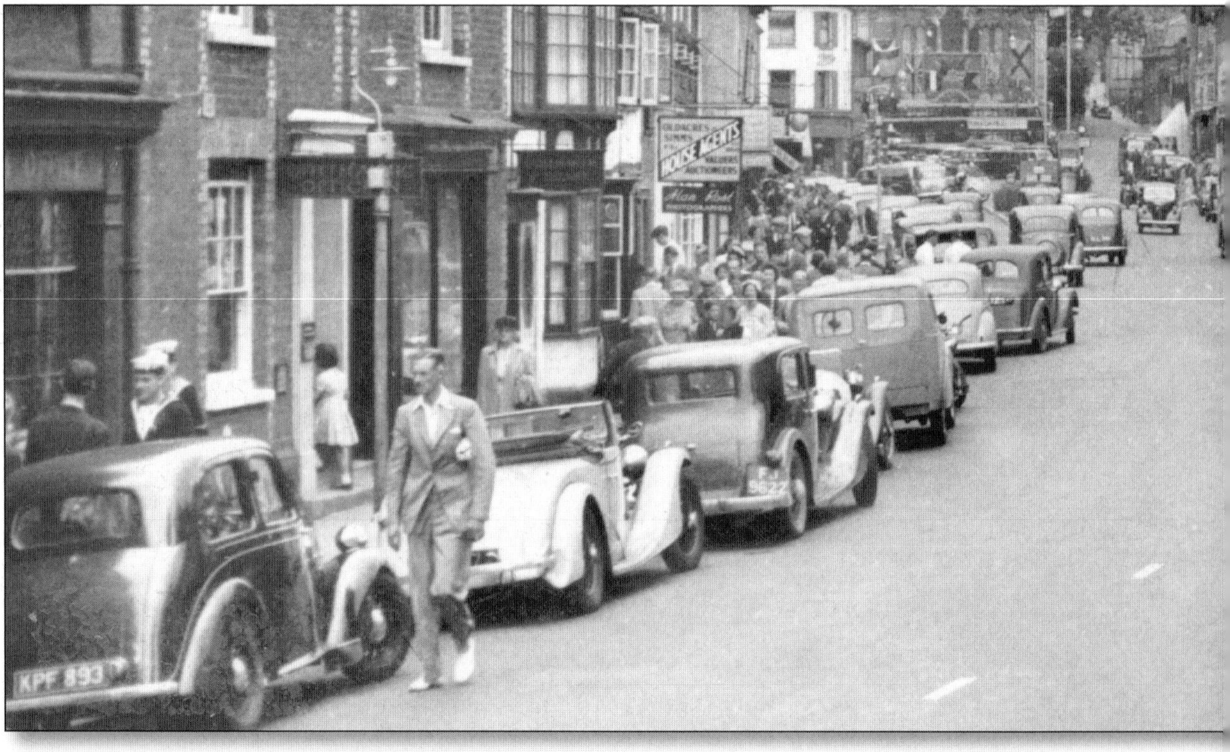

A View of the Town in the 1950s & 1960s

Left: Hart Street c1960 H73053

Below: Hart Street c1955 H73044

OTHER TOWN CENTRE STREETS

This shows the view looking along Reading Road, past the current Post Office and the Shell petrol pump, to the junction with Friday Street and into Duke Street as it heads towards the Market Place. The name Duke Street was a smartening-up of the original name, Duck Street. The houses on the left-hand side had been rebuilt further back for road widening in 1870. Photograph H73065, pages 66-67 was taken looking south along Bell Street as it curves towards the Market Place cross-roads. Opposite the fine Georgian house with the modillion cornice was Simmons and Sons which is now the entrance to Waitrose supermarket and a backland car park. At the time of this photograph, the over-scaled 1937 Regal Cinema was set back in the gap by Tesco's.

READING ROAD & DUKE STREET c1955 H73019

A View of the Town in the 1950s & 1960s

Many guide books refer to the Kenton Theatre as the fourth oldest in England; but this is arguable, as its first life as a theatre was only from 1805 until 1813. After that it became a nonconformist Independent Chapel until the 1830s. It revived as a theatre briefly in the 1930s, and reopened fully in 1951. It has a proscenium arch designed by John Piper, who lived and worked in nearby Fawley across the county boundary in Buckinghamshire. Thus this addition to the town's cultural life revived just before the Frith photographers came here; it thrives to this day.

The town shown in the 1950s and 1960s views has smartened up considerably since then, but these views give a snapshot of the town before the motor car and road transport really took off. At that time, many visited the town by train, and people came for shopping and social occasions by bus. Most families had only one car, and the explosion which swamped the town in middle class Volvo estates in the 1980s and four-wheel-drive cars now had yet to happen. The 1960s were really the beginning of the untold prosperity that has reached most people by the 1980s, and by that time Henley was already a prosperous and predominantly middle class shopping centre and town. This was reflected then in the wide range of shops, and even more so now, with supermarkets for bulk shopping and the town centre for speciality shopping. The modern town is indeed in good heart.

EXTRACT FROM BARBER'S GAZETTEER OF ENGLAND & WALES 1895

The town has been thought by some antiquaries to occupy the site of the Roman station Calleva, has yielded numerous Roman coins, does not appear on record till after the time of the Norman conquest ... presents now a modern appearance, and contains a large number of handsome villa residences.

Right: BELL STREET c1965 H73065

Below: BELL STREET c1965 H73066

Below Right: THE OBELISK c1965 H73067

NORTHFIELD END

At the north end of the town the greenery is now less; the hedges on the right have been replaced by walls. The buildings remain largely unaltered. In the distance, the junction of Marlow Road and the Nettlebed Road, the start of the Fair Mile, is marked by the 18th-century obelisk in front of Clare Cottage; the obelisk has by now lost the bracket lamps we saw in the 1893 view earlier in the book. A few years later, in 1970, the obelisk was moved again, this time away from the traffic into Marshmill Meadows.

Ordnance Survey Map

Ordnance Survey Map

An Ordnance Survey Map Showing Henley-on-Thames and Surrounding areas 1910

THE 1890 REGATTA

This view and 27204, pages 72-73 are well away from the town; the banks are consequently more thinly populated and the boats, punts and skiffs far fewer than one might expect. At the right in both views is Temple Island, the start of the course, with its garden temple by James Wyatt, erected in 1771 as a fishing lodge for Sambrook Freeman of Fawley Court. It and the island are now owned by the Henley Royal Regatta, and the temple has recently been well restored.

Right: THE REGATTA 1890 27205

Below: details from left to right:
THE REGATTA 1890 27204

THE REGATTA 1890 27203

THE BRIDGE 1899 43016

REGATTA DAY 1899 43020

The Regatta Town

When Frith's photographer, picking his way through the carriages and crowds, arrived in Henley to record the 1890 Regatta, it had already been an annual event since the early years of Queen Victoria's reign. The idea of rowing races had really got off the ground in 1829, when the very first Oxford and Cambridge boat race was held here. The course chosen ran from Hambleden past Temple Island to Henley. The stretch from Temple Island to the town is straight and wide, and the popularity of the University race set men thinking. A public meeting in March 1839 was held in the Town Hall; it was presided over by Thomas Stonor of nearby Stonor Park, later to be Lord Camoys.

Among the crucial decisions taken was that the race should be upstream, against the river flow, so that the townspeople could see the finish and, more importantly, benefit economically from the crowds. The start was to be at Temple Island on the Fawley Court estate (the temple was a fishing lodge designed by James Wyatt in 1771). The meeting agreed the prize money and authorised the cup and medal designs, which were all to be funded by public subscription. The first Regatta was held on 14 June 1839. There were four races and seven entries — it took only three hours. Trinity College, Cambridge won the Grand Challenge Cup, and the Wave Crew won the Town Challenge Cup. From these small beginnings the regatta, held in the twenty-seventh week of each year, grew to be the essential lifeblood of the town after its loss of the coaching and river commerce to the railways.

The regatta grew spectacularly: in 1851 Prince Albert became its Patron, and it assumed its present title of the Henley Royal Regatta. The branch railway arrived in 1857. Numerous special trains were laid on for regatta week, packed with ladies in their finery and big hats and with gentlemen in striped blazers and straw boaters or rowing caps. Carriages lined the river bridge, and the banks along the course were crowded with luxurious houseboats.

THE REGATTA 1890 27204

THE REGATTA 1890 27202

This view gives some idea of the scrum of small boats that reluctantly cleared the course while a race was under way; they were the subject of Punch cartoons, outraged commentary and standing jokes. In 1899 booms were placed to fence in the course and protect it from stray spectator boats, and nowadays the course is much better marshalled. On the left are the then brand-new range of boathouses built by Hobbs and Sons, while beyond are wharves and boatbuilders' sheds, soon to be replaced by houses.

The Regatta Town

The Regatta 1890 27203

In 1888 there were no less than 88 houseboats and 55 launches moored along the river banks. Some houseboats, with their sheltered upper deck viewing galleries, and occasionally equipped with grand pianos, had up to twelve beds below decks, and even separate kitchen and servants' boats tied up nearby. The houseboats also lined the banks as far south as Marsh Lock. They are now a thing of the past. Besides the houseboats, the river itself was a scrum of small boats. Rowing boats, skiffs, punts, steam launches - every kind and size jostled for position, crossing the course and generally milling about. 'See and be seen' was always the motto for the fashionable crowds (it still is).

The modern regatta has numerous marquees and temporary stands in the meadows alongside the course, and there are far fewer private boats getting in the way. The racing is a serious business - and so is the eating and drinking and socialising. Since 1886 the races have finished opposite Phyllis Court to avoid the tight bend at Poplar Point, which always gave the crew rowing on the Berkshire side an unfair advantage, as the bend swings east. The name 'Poplar Point' commemorates the Lombardy poplars planted by Field Marshal Conway in the late 18th century; they were among the first planted in England, but were felled in the 1860s and 1870s. The views in this book show their replacements, black poplars.

HOUSEBOATS AND FLOATING PALACES

This view was taken looking along the river towards Temple Island with a race under way. This far from town, the small boats are less numerous, and the views from the houseboats are less impeded. Bright with flags, pennants and awnings, they made a striking sight; there were nearly a hundred of them by the late 1890s.

Moving the finish line was unpopular with town traders, but their fears were unjustified. The event has hardly diminished in its appeal since 1895, when Emily Climenson records that 34,142 Regatta-goers arrived by train alone. Anyone who has tried to drive through Henley during Regatta week will know that the event attracts countless cars. An indication of its worldwide popularity is that in 1999 eighty-six foreign crews competed, which is something of an increase over the first two, who arrived in 1878. These were American university crews, who were followed by a German university crew in 1880 and by other nations after that. Indeed, the course was used for the Olympic Games in 1908 and again in 1948: the ultimate accolade.

From its first three-hour event, the Regatta rapidly grew to a week-long series of races; it is now one of the key events in the English social calendar. What with champagne picnics and competition for stewards' enclosure tickets; a cynic might describe the Regatta as hospitality tents with a bit of rowing attached. Indeed, Emily Climenson herself back in 1896 described it as 'this world celebrated water-picnic'. She went on to give a pen portrait of the oarsmen and other more stalwart visitors. Bursting with swooning, patriotic pride, she wrote: 'no other event in England will give a foreigner such an opportunity of noting the muscular physique of John Bull, from the young-limbed athlete hardly in his twenties, to the middle-aged man, his hair perhaps flecked with grey, but with muscles of iron, the hero of endless feats of strength, and still ready for more!'

Now the Henley Royal Regatta owns Temple Island, various riverside meadows, the fine headquarters building by the bridge (a classically-inspired building by Terry Farrell opened in 1986), and Bridge House behind it, as well as other parcels of land; while the equally prestigious Leander Rowing Club has its headquarters near the north side of the bridge. The Regatta now has eighteen major events. For those who wish to know more, I urge you to visit the excellent River and Rowing Museum in Mill Meadows, opened in 1998 in a superb building by David Chipperfield reminiscent of timber boathouses.

EXTRACT FROM BARBER'S GAZETTEER OF ENGLAND & WALES 1895

The event of all others, however, which serves to make the name of Henley famous, is its annual regatta, which is universally admitted to take the first place among the amateur aquatic contests of England. It usually takes place about the beginning of July, and it attracts the best amateur oarsmen of England and occasionally some from the Continent, while it almost ranks with Ascot as a meeting-place of the fashionable world.

The Regatta Town

THE 1899 REGATTA

All three views taken by the Frith photographer in 1899 are south of the Regatta course, which from 1886 had its finishing line near Phyllis Court. In the first view (right) we are looking towards the bridge from south Riverside and the second (bottom right) was taken from the bridge itself. The third (bottom left) was taken looking along Riverside north with the gardens of the Red Lion on the right; this was a most exclusive seating area, but it has since been lost to road improvements. In this view we see the black poplars on the Berkshire bank which replaced the late 18th-century ones planted by Field Marshal Conway.

EXTRACT FROM BARBER'S GAZETTEER OF ENGLAND & WALES 1895

The environs are very beautiful, and comprise one of the finest reaches of the Thames, flanked by gentle hills or cliffs covered with hanging woods.

Right: The Bridge 1899 43016

Below: Regatta Day 1899 43020

Below Right: Regatta Day 1899 43019

THE REGATTA TOWN

THE REGATTA IN THE 1950S

Both views are from the Berkshire bank. One was taken looking towards the bridge; the other was taken looking north-east to the finishing line. On the Henley bank we can see the old 1913 grandstand with a glimpse of Phyllis Court in the trees behind. The grandstand was rebuilt in 1993.

Above: THE TOW PATH c1955 H73048

Below: THE BRIDGE c1955 H73046

A Brief Excursion Along the River

No town can be isolated from its hinterland, and Henley with its position on the banks of the River Thames is no exception. Fawley Court, for example, a mile or so downstream, is inextricably linked into Henley's history, not only for its Temple Island and grounds used for the Henley Royal Regatta, but also for the influence over the town of the families that lived there. The owners of Fawley Court were normally Lords of the Manor of Henley, despite the fact that Fawley Court is mostly (since 1992 entirely) over the county boundary in Buckinghamshire. In the 17th century the Whitelocks owned at one time or another not only Fawley Court, but also Phyllis Court between it and Henley, Henley Park, and Greenlands. Fawley and Henley had an eventful Civil War in the 1640s: the town in effect guarded the west flank of Parliamentary territory while the King was based in Oxford.

On the Berkshire side, south of the bridge and occupying the ridge, Park Place has also played an important role in the history of Henley, particularly during the life of Field Marshal Henry Conway. He had bought the estate in 1752 from the executors of the late Prince of Wales. His daughter, the Hon Mrs Ann Damer, was later the sculptor of the keystones of the bridge. The mansion had a superb location atop the plateau and 200 feet above the river; it was enlarged by the Field Marshal, but his most notable contribution was to the landscaping of the 900-acre park. He imported a 'Druidic Temple', in fact a stone circle, from Jersey in 1787, which was given to him when he was Governor of Jersey. The Field Marshal made many other improvements before his death in 1795, planting trees and adding garden buildings. Happy Valley was a particularly successful piece of work. The valley leads down to the river bank; at the top is a gigantic grotto with six vaulted chambers, which is said to have been built

Marsh Lock From below the Mills 1890 27187

MARSH MILLS AND MARSH LOCKS

Marsh Mills, a mile upstream from Henley bridge, had long ground the corn brought to Henley market, returning it as meal and flour for transhipment to London and elsewhere. The Mills are seen beyond the moored houseboat: they have two identical bays with bag hoist projections in each gable. The building is long gone, along with Henley's corn trade, and has been replaced by a 1960s block of flats which straddles the old mill race.

using stonework salvaged from the ruins of medieval Reading Abbey. An estate road passes under the Henley-Wargrave Road to reach the river, where the Victorian boathouse and lodge were built in 1847. Sad to say, Conway's mansion was demolished in 1869 and replaced by the present Italianate one in 1870, a much larger house.

The Wargrave road bridge was made into an ornamental rustic one clad in boulders and large stone; hence its first names, the Cyclopic Bridge or the Ragged Arches. It is now known as Conway Bridge. It was well described by Horace Walpole in 1763: 'the works at Park Place go on bravely ... the bridge sublime, composed of loose rocks that appear to have been tumbled together there, the very wreck of the Deluge. One stone is of 14 hundredweight!' It was rumoured that the boulders came from the ruins of Reading Abbey, but in fact the builders scoured fourteen counties for them; the bridge eventually cost the staggering sum of £2,000. It still carries modern traffic, so it must have been well wrought. Field Marshal Conway did much on the advice of the Reverend Humphrey Gainsborough, who arrived in Henley as minister of the Congregational Church in 1748. He was the brother of Thomas, one of England's finest artists, and an enthusiastic amateur engineer and designer. He worked on Conway Bridge and is thought to have been responsible for its design and engineering, and he made the White Hill causeway on the Berkshire side.

Gainsborough also engaged himself in improving the Thames navigation. After objections by the Commissioners of the Thames to a clergyman being on the committee, he virtually took over the conversion of the dangerous flash locks to the much more satisfactory pound locks. He was also responsible for the reconstruction of the locks between Marlow and Sonning. His success in the project led to his being appointed collector of tolls for the locks between Hambleden and Sonning. One wonders how he found time to minister to his congregation (so, incidentally, did the great founder of Methodism, John Wesley, who visited the town on a number of occasions). Marsh Lock was completed in 1772, although it has been completely rebuilt several times since, most recently in 1998; its gates are now electrically operated. Humphrey Gainsborough would have been most interested in such a development.

Flash locks had gates at one end of the lock only, so when the gates were opened the barge or boat was 'flashed' through; this could be a highly hazardous process, and many scores of bargemen were

MARSH LOCK c1955 H73052

MARSH MILLS AND MARSH LOCKS

New Mills are on the Oxfordshire bank. The lock was a flash lock until Humphrey Gainsborough replaced it by a pound lock in 1772, bypassing the weir. The rendered house with flanking bay windows is the miller's house, Marsh Mills House.

drowned and boats lost over the years. Marsh Flash Lock is seen in one of Siberechts' 1690 paintings. To get back upstream, a barge had to be hauled on ropes by a capstan; the last capstan, for the former Hurley flash lock, survives at Wittington, now restored by Wycombe District Council. A pound lock has gates at each end, so one set of gates is opened and the water raised or lowered to that of the upstream or downstream river level. When the water in the lock is level, the gates are opened, and the barge or boat proceeds safely on its way - a much less chancy business all together. Nowadays the locks are mainly used by leisure craft, but when the locks were completed in the 1770s their purpose was to help the river trade of barges and other cargo-carrying river craft.

Marsh Mill was crucial to the economy of Henley until the decline of the river trade, for it was at these watermills that the corn and grain from the Chiltern Hills and the Berkshire cornfields was ground. The meal and flour was then brought to the town wharves, usually on wagons and across the bridge, for transport on to London and other markets. After the bridge was rebuilt in 1785, the miller was exempted from the bridge toll for his grain and flour wagons, although it cost him a fee of £4 a year. As this was considerably cheaper than paying the toll in the normal way, it gives some indication of the scale of Marsh Mills business. Indeed, in the 1720s about three hundred cartloads of corn were often sold on a single Thursday market day, and most of it was subsequently ground at Marsh Mill. There are some views of Marsh Lock and the former mill in this chapter.

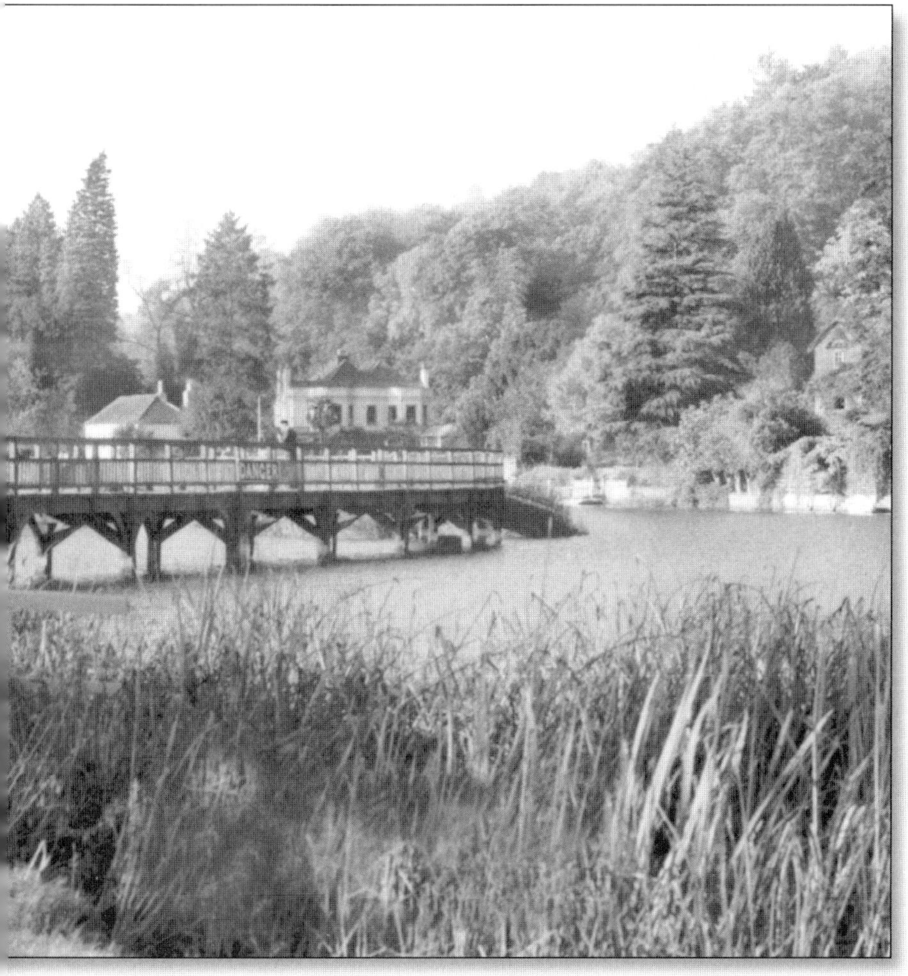

Left:
MARSH LOCK c1955 H73504

Below Left:
MARSH WEIR c1955 H73049

Below:
BOATHOUSES 1893 31750

PARK PLACE

Field Marshal Conway's great 18th-century landscape improvements and garden buildings in the grounds of Park Place included the rustic boulder-bedecked bridge on the right, carrying the Wargrave Road over his drive to the river bank. The boathouse and cottage on the left were built in 1847, long after his death, in cottage orné style for the then owner, the Earl of Malmesbury.

Names of Subscribers

The following people have kindly supported this book by purchasing limited edition copies prior to publication.

In memory of Florence Andrews

Norman and Elizabeth Attrill

The Family Beckett

Lavinia Bolton

Gary C Broad

J D Brown, Henley-on-Thames

Peter J Bush, Shiplake

The Chiswell Family, Checkendon

The Cilliers Family, Henley-on-Thames

Pam Cole

George and Sheila Constantinidi, Marsh Mills

Tony and Audrey Cooke, Henley-on-Thames

Mr and Mrs Michael Cooper and Children

Mr R and Mrs M de Board

Ann K Dowling, Henley-on-Thames

B R Eastick

Ann and Chris Eggleton and Family, Henley

To David Eggleton, love Mum

John and Nora French, Henley-on-Thames

The Garland Family, Binfield Heath

The Glithro Family, Emmer Green, Reading

Andrew and Judith Harwood, Belmont, Surrey

Henley Royal Regatta

Mike Hornsby, love from Lindy and Bevan

Roger Howarth, Henley Grammar School 1964 - 72

Antony and Lauren Hunt, Henley-on-Thames

Paul and Sue Ilett, Henley-on-Thames

Richard Jones

Happy times, beautiful home, the Keatings

Robin and Janet Laye, Henley, Oxon

In memory of Gordon and James Leighton

The Lovells of Henley-on-Thames

The McCormack Family

Christine and David McKnight

Rowena McMenamin

David Mole, Henley-on-Thames

Arabella Napier, Henley-on-Thames and USA

Mr D A and Mrs E M Napier, Henley

Mary Norris

Colin Patrick

As a tribute to my parents, Gordon Pike

Antonia Richards

Angus Robertson

Colin Rocke

The Rowlett Family, Lower Shiplake

Elizabeth and Francis Sheppard

Ellen Tame

In memory of J J Tame, Marsh Lock-Keeper

Alison Tapp - Lover of Henley

Christopher Tapp - Henley Man

Irene and David Tapp, Henley-on-Thames

Mr A G Taylor

Mr Keith Thomas Thatcher, Henley

Mr D Trimmings, Henley-on-Thames

Jasmine Weaver, Henley-on-Thames

In memory of Richard Ian Wilson, Highmoor

Roswitha and Arnold Zarach and Family

Index

The Francis Frith Collection Titles

www.francisfrith.co.uk

The Francis Frith Collection publishes over 100 new titles each year. A selection of those currently available is listed below. For latest catalogue please contact The Francis Frith Collection. ***Town Books*** 96 pages, approximately 75 photos. ***County and Themed Books*** 128 pages, approximately 135 photos (unless specified).

Accrington Old and New
Alderley Edge and Wilmslow
Amersham, Chesham and Rickmansworth
Andover
Around Abergavenny
Around Alton
Aylesbury
Barnstaple
Bedford
Bedfordshire
Berkshire Living Memories
Berkshire Pocket Album
Blackpool Pocket Album
Bognor Regis
Bournemouth
Bradford
Bridgend
Bridport
Brighton and Hove
Bristol
Buckinghamshire
Calne Living Memories
Camberley Pocket Album
Canterbury Cathedral
Cardiff Old and New
Chatham and the Medway Towns
Chelmsford
Chepstow Then and Now
Cheshire
Cheshire Living Memories
Chester
Chesterfield
Chigwell
Christchurch
Churches of East Cornwall
Clevedon
Clitheroe
Corby Living Memories
Cornish Coast
Cornwall Living Memories
Cotswold Living Memories
Cotswold Pocket Album
Coulsdon, Chipstead and Woodmanstern
County Durham
Cromer, Sheringham and Holt
Dartmoor Pocket Album
Derby
Derbyshire
Derbyshire Living Memories
Devon
Devon Churches
Dorchester
Dorset Coast Pocket Album
Dorset Living Memories
Dorset Villages
Down the Dart
Down the Severn
Down the Thames
Dunmow, Thaxted and Finchingfield
Durham
East Anglia Pocket Album
East Devon
East Grinstead
Edinburgh
Ely and The Fens
Essex Pocket Album
Essex Second Selection
Essex: The London Boroughs
Exeter
Exmoor
Falmouth
Farnborough, Fleet and Aldershot
Folkestone
Frome
Furness and Cartmel Peninsulas
Glamorgan
Glasgow
Glastonbury
Gloucester
Gloucestershire
Greater Manchester
Guildford
Hailsham
Hampshire
Harrogate
Hastings and Bexhill
Haywards Heath Living Memories
Heads of the Valleys
Heart of Lancashire Pocket Album
Helston
Herefordshire
Horsham
Humberside Pocket Album
Huntingdon, St Neots and St Ives
Hythe, Romney Marsh and Ashford
Ilfracombe
Ipswich Pocket Album
Isle of Wight
Isle of Wight Living Memories
King's Lynn
Kingston upon Thames
Lake District Pocket Album
Lancashire Living Memories
Lancashire Villages

Available from your local bookshop or from the publisher

The Francis Frith Collection Titles (continued)

Lancaster, Morecambe and Heysham Pocket Album
Leeds Pocket Album
Leicester
Leicestershire
Lincolnshire Living Memoires
Lincolnshire Pocket Album
Liverpool and Merseyside
London Pocket Album
Ludlow
Maidenhead
Maidstone
Malmesbury
Manchester Pocket Album
Marlborough
Matlock
Merseyside Living Memories
Nantwich and Crewe
New Forest
Newbury Living Memories
Newquay to St Ives
North Devon Living Memories
North London
North Wales
North Yorkshire
Northamptonshire
Northumberland
Northwich
Nottingham
Nottinghamshire Pocket Album
Oakham
Odiham Then and Now
Oxford Pocket Album
Oxfordshire
Padstow
Pembrokeshire
Penzance
Petersfield Then and Now
Plymouth
Poole and Sandbanks
Preston Pocket Album
Ramsgate Old and New
Reading Pocket Album
Redditch Living Memories
Redhill to Reigate
Richmond
Ringwood
Rochdale
Romford Pocket Album
Salisbury Pocket Album
Scotland
Scottish Castles
Sevenoaks and Tonbridge
Sheffield and South Yorkshire Pocket Album
Shropshire
Somerset
South Devon Coast
South Devon Living Memories
South East London
Southampton Pocket Album
Southend Pocket Album
Southport
Southwold to Aldeburgh
Stourbridge Living Memories
Stratford upon Avon
Stroud
Suffolk
Suffolk Pocket Album
Surrey Living Memories
Sussex
Sutton
Swanage and Purbeck
Swansea Pocket Album
Swindon Living Memories
Taunton
Teignmouth
Tenby and Saundersfoot
Tiverton
Torbay
Truro
Uppingham
Villages of Kent
Villages of Surrey
Villages of Sussex Pocket Album
Wakefield and the Five Towns Living Memories
Warrington
Warwick
Warwickshire Pocket Album
Wellingborough Living Memories
Wells
Welsh Castles
West Midlands Pocket Album
West Wiltshire Towns
West Yorkshire
Weston-super-Mare
Weymouth
Widnes and Runcorn
Wiltshire Churches
Wiltshire Living Memories
Wiltshire Pocket Album
Wimborne
Winchester Pocket Album
Windermere
Windsor
Wirral
Wokingham and Bracknell
Woodbridge
Worcester
Worcestershire
Worcestershire Living Memories
Wyre Forest
York Pocket Album
Yorkshire
Yorkshire Coastal Memories
Yorkshire Dales
Yorkshire Revisited

Frith Products & Services

Francis Frith would doubtless be pleased to know that the pioneering publishing venture he started in 1860 still continues today. Over a hundred and forty years later, The Francis Frith Collection continues in the same innovative tradition and is now one of the foremost publishers of vintage photographs in the world. Some of the current activities include:

Interior Decoration

Today Frith's photographs can be seen framed and as giant wall murals in thousands of pubs, restaurants, hotels, banks, retail stores and other public buildings throughout the country. In every case they enhance the unique local atmosphere of the places they depict and provide reminders of gentler days in an increasingly busy and frenetic world.

Product Promotions

Frith products are used by many major companies to promote the sales of their own products or to reinforce their own history and heritage. Frith promotions have been used by Hovis bread, Courage beers, Scots Porage Oats, Colman's mustard, Cadbury's foods, Mellow Birds coffee, Dunhill pipe tobacco, Guinness, and Bulmer's Cider.

Genealogy and Family History

As the interest in family history and roots grows world-wide, more and more people are turning to Frith's photographs of Great Britain for images of the towns, villages and streets where their ancestors lived; and, of course, photographs of the churches and chapels where their ancestors were christened, married and buried are an essential part of every genealogy tree and family album.

Frith Products

All Frith photographs are available Framed or just as Mounted Prints and Posters (size 23 x 16 inches). These may be ordered from the address below. From time to time other products - Address Books, Calendars, Table Mats, etc - are available.

The Internet

Already ninety thousand Frith photographs can be viewed and purchased on the internet through the Frith websites and a myriad of partner sites.

For more detailed information on Frith companies and products, look at these sites:

www.francisfrith.co.uk
www.francisfrith.com
(for North American visitors)

See the complete list of Frith Books at:
www.francisfrith.co.uk
This web site is regularly updated with the latest list of publications from The Francis Frith Collection. If you wish to buy books relating to another part of the country that your local bookshop does not stock, you may purchase on-line.

For further information, trade, or author enquiries please contact us at the address below:

The Francis Frith Collection, Frith's Barn, Teffont, Salisbury, Wiltshire, England SP3 5QP.
Tel: +44 (0)1722 716 376 Fax: +44 (0)1722 716 881 Email: sales@francisfrith.co.uk

See Frith books on the internet at www.francisfrith.co.uk

FREE PRINT OF YOUR CHOICE

Mounted Print
Overall size 14 x 11 inches (355 x 280mm)

Choose any Frith photograph in this book. Simply complete the Voucher opposite and return it with your remittance for £2.25 (to cover postage and handling) and we will print the photograph of your choice in SEPIA (size 11 x 8 inches) and supply it in a cream mount with a burgundy rule line (overall size 14 x 11 inches). **Please note: photographs with a reference number starting with a "Z" are not Frith photographs and cannot be supplied under this offer. Offer valid for delivery to one UK address only.**

***PLUS:* Order additional Mounted Prints at HALF PRICE - £7.49 each** (normally £14.99) If you would like to order more Frith prints from this book, possibly as gifts for friends and family, you can buy them at half price (with no additional postage and handling costs).

***PLUS:* Have your Mounted Prints framed**
For an extra £14.95 per print you can have your mounted print(s) framed in an elegant polished wood and gilt moulding, overall size 16 x 13 inches (no additional postage and handling required).

IMPORTANT!

These special prices are only available if you use this form to order. You must use the ORIGINAL VOUCHER on this page (no copies permitted). We can only despatch to one UK address. This offer cannot be combined with any other offer.

Send completed Voucher form to:
The Francis Frith Collection, Frith's Barn, Teffont, Salisbury, Wiltshire SP3 5QP

CHOOSE A PHOTOGRAPH FROM THIS BOOK

Please do not photocopy this voucher. Only the original is valid, so please fill it in, cut it out and return it to us with your order.

Picture ref no	Page no	Qty	Mounted @ £7.49	Framed + £14.95	Total Cost £
		1	Free of charge*	£	£
			£7.49	£	£
			£7.49	£	£
			£7.49	£	£
			£7.49	£	£
			£7.49	£	£
Please allow 28 days for delivery. Offer available to one UK address only			* Post & handling		£2.25
			Total Order Cost		£

Title of this book ....
I enclose a cheque/postal order for £ ....
made payable to 'The Francis Frith Collection'

OR please debit my Mastercard / Visa / Maestro / Amex card, details below

Card Number

Issue No (Maestro only) Valid from (Maestro)

Expires Signature

Name Mr/Mrs/Ms ....
Address ....
....
....
.... Postcode ....
Daytime Tel No ....
Email ....

ISBN 1-85937-990-7 Valid to 31/12/08

Free Print - see overleaf

Can you help us with information about any of the Frith photographs in this book?

We are gradually compiling an historical record for each of the photographs in the Frith archive. It is always fascinating to find out the names of the people shown in the pictures, as well as insights into the shops, buildings and other features depicted.

If you recognize anyone in the photographs in this book, or if you have information not already included in the author's caption, do let us know. We would love to hear from you, and will try to publish it in future books or articles.

Our production team

Frith books are produced by a small dedicated team at offices in the converted Grade II listed 18th-century barn at Teffont near Salisbury, illustrated above. Most have worked with the Frith Collection for many years. All have in common one quality: they have a passion for the Frith Collection. The team is constantly expanding, but currently includes:

Paul Baron, Jason Buck, John Buck, Heather Crisp, David Davies, Louis du Mont, Isobel Hall, Lucy Hart, Julian Hight, Peter Horne, James Kinnear, Karen Kinnear, Tina Leary, Stuart Login, Sue Molloy, Sarah Roberts, Kate Rotondetto, Dean Scource, Eliza Sackett, Terence Sackett, Sandra Sampson, Adrian Sanders, Sandra Sanger, Julia Skinner, Miles Smith, Lewis Taylor, Shelley Tolcher, Lorraine Tuck, Miranda Tunnicliffe, David Turner and Ricky Williams.